GCSE History

The USA 1919–1941

Aaron Wilkes

OXFORD

UNIVERSITY PRESS

OXFORD
UNIVERSITY PRESS

Great Clarendon Street, Oxford OX2 6DP

Oxford University Press is a department of the University of Oxford.
It furthers the University's objective of excellence in research,
scholarship, and education by publishing worldwide in

Oxford   New York

Auckland   Cape Town   Dar es Salaam   Hong Kong   Karachi
Kuala Lumpur   Madrid   Melbourne   Mexico City   Nairobi
New Delhi   Shanghai   Taipei   Toronto

With offices in

Argentina   Austria   Brazil   Chile   Czech Republic   France   Greece
Guatemala   Hungary   Italy   Japan   Poland   Portugal   Singapore
South Korea   Switzerland   Thailand   Turkey   Ukraine   Vietnam

Oxford is a registered trade mark of Oxford University Press
in the UK and in certain other countries

© Aaron Wilkes 2006

British Library Cataloguing in Publication Data

Data available

ISBN 978-1-84303-830-6

FC8307

10 9 8 7 6 5 4

Printed in China by Printplus

Paper used in the production of this book is a natural, recyclable product
made from wood grown in sustainable forests. The manufacuring process
conforms to the environmental regulations of the country of origin.

Author's acknowledgements

The author once again wishes to acknowledge Nina
Randall for her continued hard work, good humour and
advice. He would also like to thank Emma and Hannah
Wilkes, Helen Noble and John Edwards for their help,
support and encouragement during the preparation of
this book.

Editor: Nina Randall

Page design and layout: Neil Sutton, Pumpkin House,
Cambridge

Illustrations: Celia Hart

Cover design: Richard Jervis Design

Cover image: Corbis

Acknowledgements

Bettman/Corbis: 21, 24, 31, 33, 34 (right), 40, 64, 65 (both),
73, 83; Brown Brothers: 4; Charles E Rotkin/Corbis: 77; Corbis:
15, 18 (right), 26, 55 (right), 85 (both); Culver Pictures: 32,
61, 74; Franklin D Roosevelt Library Collection: 66, 71, 90;
George Eastman House, Rochester, NY: 6; Getty Images: 18
(left), 20, 29, 30 (both), 34 (left), 42, 49, 54, 56–7, 58, 62;
Mark Peterson/Corbis SABA: 23; Mary Evans/Beranger: 22;
Mary Evans Picture Library: 19, 35, 45; Peter Newark's
American Pictures: 78; ©Popperfoto.com: 50, 51, 55 (left);
Punch/Reproduced with permission of Punch Limited: 79; The
Coca-Cola Company/Image courtesy of the Advertising
Archives: 14; Time Life Pictures/Getty Images: 39; Underwood
& Underwood/Corbis: 25, 27.

'A New Deal, America 1932–45' by Josh Brooman, Longman,
2000: 61 (top left), 85; 'American Century': 70, 72; 'American
Voices': 5, 49, 77 (right); 'Buddy, can you spare a dime?' by E
Y Harburg, 1932: 57 (bottom); 'Discovering the Past: USA
between the Wars 1919–1941' by T Fiehn, R Mills, M
Samuelson and C White, John Murray, 1998: 35, 39; 88 (left);
'Don't know much about history' by Kenneth C Davis, Harper
Collins, 2003: 89 (right); 'Franklin Roosevelt' by C P Hill,
1966: 89 (left); 'From the Crash to the Blitz: 1929–1939' by C
Phillips, Macmillan, 1969: 67; 'Making History: World history
from 1914 to the Present Day' by Christopher Culpin, Collins
Educational, 1996: 86 (bottom left); 87; 'Middletown in
Transition: A Study in Cultural Conflicts' by Robert Staughton
Lynd, Helen Merrell Lynd, Harcourt, 1932: 19 (bottom left);
'Modern America' by C K MacDonald, Blackwell, 1987: 28
(left); 51, 88 (bottom right); 'Modern World History' by Kelly
and Lacy, Heinemann, 1999: 61 (bottom left); 'New Republic'
(magazine), February 1933: 56 (right); 'Seabiscuit' (film) 2003:
75; 'Strange Fruit' by Billie Holiday, 1940: 20; 'The Age of
Excess: America, 1920–32' by Josh Brooman, Longman, 1997:
18, 19 (right), 56 (top left); 'The Grapes of Wrath' by John
Steinbeck, Penguin Books Ltd, 1970: 56 (bottom left), 57
(top); 'The Memoirs of Herbert Hoover', by Herbert Hoover,
Macmillan, 1951: 61 (middle left); 'The Modern World' by
Kelly and Rees, Heinemann, 1996: 78; 'The USA: A Divided
Nation?' by Neil De Marco, Longman, 2001: 88 (top right).

Some of the exam questions have been taken from the OCR
(formerly MEG) examination papers from 1988–2005.

The wording and sentence structure of some written sources
have been adapted and simplified to make them accessible to
all students, while faithfully preserving the sense of the
original.

Contents

A land of opportunity?

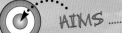

AIMS ....

The next six pages aim to show you what life was like for some of the new immigrants that chose to move to America in the early 1900s.

Try to remember:

- two reasons why immigrants moved to America;
- three facts about immigrant workers and/or the jobs they had;
- four groups that made up American society in the early 1900s.

'America will be my dreamland'

Look at **Source A** carefully. This woman has arrived by ship from Europe for a new life in America. She has all her possessions with her. A doctor is examining her eyes by lifting up her eyelids with a hook to see if she has trachoma, a blinding disease. If he thinks she is infected, she will be sent back home on the next boat. She will also be checked for other contagious diseases, hearing problems and mental illness before being allowed to sit a literacy test. All the time she runs the risk of being rejected entry into America. So what has brought this woman here? What is the attraction of a country she has never seen before, where she has no home, no work and no friends? And why did over 40 million **immigrants** like her start a new life in America between 1850 and 1919?

▼ **Source A** *These inspections took place on Ellis Island, an immigration-processing centre just a ferry ride from New York, America's biggest city. The old, ill and illiterate, as well as any suspected criminals, were sent back to their own country.*

America's newest citizens came from all over the world, but particularly from Europe. Some fled a life of poverty, famine and persecution; others were attracted by the promise of a better life. Look through **Sources B** to **F** carefully. They outline some of the reasons why so many people saw America as the 'land of opportunity'.

▼ **Source B** *A recently arrived Russian immigrant, 1909.*

"There is freedom — freedom of speech, freedom of religion and a free press. And democracy too — we will get the chance to vote. And then schooling, we have the chance to learn. No application forms, no questions asked, no entry exams, no fees. Hopefully, education will help me make pots of money, have polish on my boots, eat white bread, soup and meat. America will be my dreamland."

▼ **Source C** *The son of a Norwegian immigrant, 1919.*

"My dad came from a very poor family. His dad and grandad were both poor farmers, renting land from a huge landowner in a little spot in Norway. It was a beautiful place but we could never make enough to buy our own land. We would never have had the chance to get ahead, to make a bit more money for a better life. We had to get away."

▼ **Source D** *An advertisement for a land sale, 1880.*

Between 1850 and 1914, about 10% of the population of Europe left for a new life in America. It remains the biggest movement of people in recorded history. For some, like motor millionaire Henry Ford (son of an Irish immigrant and his Dutch wife), their experience of the new world would be a good one. For others, their new life would become a living nightmare.

> **FACT** *The American Dream?*
>
> Of the 2000 people on board *Titanic* in 1912, nearly half were migrants looking for a new life in America.

▼ **Source E** BBC TV series, *American Voices*, 2001.

> "So why choose America? … It was modern, confident, wealthy, rich in raw materials; it exported wheat, iron and steel all over the world … and America invited new immigrants to share in all this, to take a job, to pull their way up in the world."

▼ **Source F** *The immigrants' first view of America was the Statue of Liberty, situated near Ellis Island, New York. Carved at the base of the statue is a poem written in 1886:*

> "Give me your tired,
> your poor,
> your huddled
> masses yearning
> to breathe
>   free,
> the wretched
> refuse [rubbish]
> of your
>   teeming shore.
> Send these the homeless, tempest
>   [storm]-tossed to me.
> I lift my lamp beside the golden door."

WISE UP WORD

● immigrants

WORK

1 **a** Look at **Source A**. Why do you think the American government put immigrants through so many inspections and tests?

 b Do you think the tests and inspections were fair?

 c Ellis Island was nicknamed the Isle of Tears. Why do you think it got this label?

2 Look at **Source B**. Why was the writer of this source so keen to go to school?

3 Look at **Source C**. Why would this Norwegian immigrant be pleased with the poster shown in **Source D**?

4 Read the poem at the base of the Statue of Liberty (**Source F**). What is this saying about the United States?

GCSE Question time

This is a genuine question from a popular exam board. Your teacher should be able to help you to plan an answer.

● Why did immigrants see America as a 'land of opportunity'?

The immigrant experience

Source G *This photo shows an immigrant woman and her family's new apartment in New York, pictured in 1900. She had arrived by boat from Poland a few months before. What do we learn from this photograph about her life in America so far?*

▼ **Source H** *A modern historian writing about the problems faced by new immigrants.*

"Some of America's newest citizens did remarkably well and 'made good'. But more often than not, they got the worst jobs and the worst pay. They lived in the worst parts of town and came face-to-face with violent crime, drunkenness and prostitution on a daily basis."

▼ **Source I** *An Italian immigrant, 1921.*

"I was once travelling by tram home from work. It was my usual tram, packed with my fellow Italian immigrants. I saw a group of boys near the roadside and one threw a rock and smashed the window. I was showered with glass and my head started to bleed. We often got trouble on that tram — it made me feel most unwelcome."

▼ **Source J** *A Polish immigrant, 1919.*

"There is always trouble in my factory. Some don't like us new immigrants. Some say we take jobs away from true Americans and we bring down wages because we are prepared to work for less. I've had my fingers broken and my food thrown over the floor."

▼ **Source K** *Tony, a Greek-born restaurant owner, interviewed in 1939.*

"When I came here I knew nothing, couldn't even speak English. I had a terrible job as a cleaner but one day a customer asked me if I wanted to help him in his restaurant. I worked my way up, learning all the time, married an American woman and now I own my own restaurant. I'm a success — in fact, I believe any hard worker with common sense can make it here."

FACT *Dublin the numbers*

In 1920, there were twice as many Irish people in New York as there were in Dublin, Ireland's largest city. New York City contained districts – known by the names of the immigrants that dominated the area – Little Italy and Chinatown for example.

By 1920, American society was made up of more religions, more colours, more cultures and more languages than any other country in the world. For many newcomers, America was not what they expected. For others, like the man in **Source K**, America was their dreamland. Clearly, every immigrant's experience was different. By the early 1920s, the government began cutting down on the number of immigrants by introducing new laws, which limited the amount of new arrivals. The 1921 Immigration Quota Law allowed only 350 000 immigrants to enter America each year. This was cut to 150 000 by 1929. It seemed as if America's 'open door' for immigrants was beginning to shut!

WORK

1 a Look at **Sources G** and **H**. What do these sources tell us about life in America for many new immigrants?
   b Why do you think so many new immigrants to America ended up in the poorer, slum areas of towns and cities?

2 Look at **Sources I** and **J**. Why do you think these immigrants faced such hostility?

3 Look at **Source K**. If the restaurant owner in this source could use three words or phrases to describe his personal experience of American life, what might they be? Write them down and explain why you chose each word or phrase.

4 a America's policy of allowing so much immigration between 1850 and 1920 is often called an 'open door policy'. What do you think this label means?
   b Is this an accurate label to use after 1920? Give reasons for your answer.

The melting pot

America is a huge country – about 40 times the size of the UK. By 1920, there were over 100 different nationalities living there, contributing to a population of over 120 million. Immigration had made the USA a very mixed society!

Some people said that America was like a vast 'melting pot' of different races, cultures and religions. So how did some of the newest immigrants cope? And who exactly were the 'Americans'?

The first Americans

Sometimes known as Native Americans or 'Red Indians', the first Americans lived in tribes across America for thousands of years before white men arrived to live there. Gradually, white settlers from Europe took their land and forced them to live in special areas called reservations.

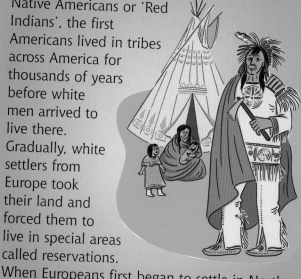

When Europeans first began to settle in North America, there were as many as five million native Americans. By 1900, there were about 250 000.

Old immigrants

Large groups of white settlers began to arrive from Europe in the 1600s, particularly from Britain, Holland and Germany. These settlers fought many wars between them-selves and with the Native Americans who had lived there for thousands of years. Soon, the largest group

of white settlers, the British, began to regard America as part of the British Empire. After about 150 years, the descendants of the early settlers started to hate being ruled from Britain. They fought, and won, a War of Independence against the British and America became an independent country. By the 1900s, white English-speakers had become the most powerful group in America. They tended to hold the best jobs, have the most money and political power. All the American presidents were white English-speakers! Surveys showed that about 10% of American people owned 90% of the country's wealth. No prizes for guessing which group in American society made up the top 10% – that's right, the old immigrants!

Black Americans

Millions of African men, women and children were taken to work as slaves on huge cotton and tobacco farms in America between 1600 and 1800. Slavery ended in 1865 and the slaves were set free but many remained near the farms to work. By 1920, there were about ten million Black Americans. They still had limited freedom, including no right to vote.

▶ **_Source L_** *The Great Seal or Coat of Arms of America. The motto 'E pluribus unum' means 'from the many: one'.*

New immigrants

A wave of new immigrants flooded into America from about 1850 onwards. They came mainly from eastern and southern Europe – Russia, Poland, Italy, Hungary, Czechoslovakia and Greece, for example. Over one million people left Ireland for America after major famines between 1845 and 1848. There was also a growing number of Chinese and Japanese immigrants. Mexicans, Cubans and others from South America – collectively known as Hispanics – moved across the border for a new life too. Some people saw the new immigrants as a threat to their way of life!

WORK

1 **a** Write a sentence or two about each of these different groups that made up American society in the 1920s: • first Americans • old immigrants • Black Americans • new immigrants

   b Which group do you think were happiest in the 1920s? Give reasons for your answer.

   c Which group do you think was most unhappy about their life in America? Explain your answer.

   d Why was American society known as 'the melting pot' in the 1920s?

2 Look at **Source L**.

   a Why do you think the motto 'E pluribus unum' was chosen?

   b Do <u>you</u> think <u>all</u> people living in America in the 1920s were happy with the motto? Think carefully about what the motto means and give reasons for your answer.

3 Use the evidence on pages 4–9 to write a letter home as if you were an immigrant to America in the 1920s. In your letter, mention: arriving at Ellis Island, your reasons for leaving your home country, your experiences of New York, your opinion of your new life and hopes for the future. Plan your letter first and discuss your work with a partner.

Who runs what?

AIMS

These two pages look at the way America is governed.
Aim to:
- know the difference between state and central government;
- understand what the Bill of Rights and the US Constitution are.

When British settlers first went to live in America, they established 13 different regions or living areas along America's east coast. The settlers were mostly farmers and grew crops like tobacco and cotton. Gradually, over many years, the British settlers began to see themselves as Americans and got fed up with British control and taxation. On 4 July 1777, the 13 colonies decided they no longer wanted to be part of the British Empire and declared their independence. The British sent soldiers over the Atlantic Ocean to sort out the American rebels and force them to stay loyal to Britain. They met fierce resistance and, after a long war, the Americans won their independence and the right to run their own country. The Americans joined their 13 colonies (or 'states' as they are now called) together to form the United States of America. George Washington was their first President and their capital city was named after him. The first ever flag of the USA was made up of 13 stars and 13 stripes. Today, the number of stripes remains the same but there are now 50 stars representing the 50 states.

After winning their independence, the Americans drew up a set of rules – a **constitution** – describing how the country should be governed.

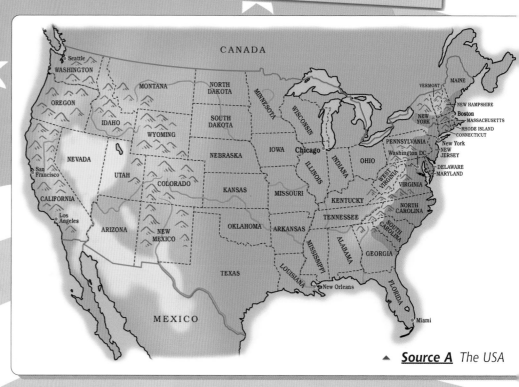

▲ **Source A** The USA

It was decided that there should be two types of government. The *central* (sometimes called 'federal') government, based in Washington DC, would control things that affected the *whole* country (like foreign affairs, the army and the postal service). A *state* government would also operate in each individual state and would make laws that applied to their own state only.

Central government was to be made up of a president (elected every four years), a cabinet of advisors and **Congress** (like a parliament) made up of elected people from the different states.

The American people could also vote for their state government, with each state having its own laws, its own police and court system, and its own governor in charge. Convicted murderers, for example, may receive the death penalty in some states but be sentenced to life imprisonment in others. Further, the police of one state could not chase a criminal across 'state-lines' into another state. Only the FBI (Federal Bureau of Investigation) could cross state borders whilst attempting to solve very serious 'federal crimes' or catch criminals who had committed crimes in more than one state.

▼ **Source B** *The first part of the American Constitution was the Bill of Rights. However, some states found ways to get around offering these rights to everyone and, by 1919, many states refused to recognise the right to vote of women, Black Americans and Native Americans.*

BILL OF RIGHTS

The American government has guaranteed that its people have the right to vote. There are also other rights and freedoms. They include:

- Freedom of speech (people can say what they want – within reason!);

- Freedom of belief (people can worship who they want);

- Freedom of information (the right to read and listen to what they want);

- Freedom in law (the right to a fair trial, freedom from unfair arrest);

- Freedom of assembly (the right to meet in groups);

- Freedom of protection (the right to carry a weapon to protect yourself – which is why licensed guns are legal in America).

WISE UP WORDS

- constitution   Democratic Party   Congress
  Republican Party   laissez faire

FACT   *Vote for me!*

Voters had two main political parties to choose from:

- The **Republican Party** liked to preserve traditions and stay out of people's lives wherever possible (a policy called **laissez faire**, a French phrase meaning 'leave alone'). They didn't believe in high taxes – which pleased rich people and businessmen!

- The **Democratic Party** was more of an ordinary people's party, preferring to intervene in everyday life if it were needed. They favoured helping those in need – the poor or elderly for example.

The Democrats had more support in the southern states (where there were more poor people), whilst the Republicans had more support in the north (where there were more industries, more jobs and more wealth). Democrats were seen by many as more liberal (prepared to change things); Republicans were seen as more conservative (traditional).

WORK

1   **a**   Why do Americans today celebrate 'Independence Day' on 4 July each year?

    b   Explain why today's American flag has 50 stars and 13 stripes.

2   **a**   Draw this puzzle into your book and fill in the answers to the clues.

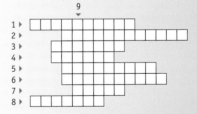

    1   One of the two main political parties.

    2   Set of rules describing how America should be governed.

    3   Also known as 'Federal' government.

    4   Bill of _____.

    5   Elected every four years.

    6   The other main political party.

    7   Each one has its own laws, police force and courts.

    8   Republicans like to 'leave alone'.

    b   Now read *down* the puzzle (clue 9). Write a sentence or two about this word.

The richest country in the world

AIMS ....

After completing the work over the next four pages, you should be able to:

- explain how different factors helped America become the richest country in the world;
- identify different groups that didn't make lots of money in the 1920s.

In 1926, the American government announced that American workers were earning, on average, nearly twice as much money as any other workers in any other country in the world. They said that the standard of living in the USA was the highest it had ever been in the country's history – Americans were officially the richest people in the world! So why had people started to earn more than ever before? What sort of things were Americans making – and buying – in such huge numbers? And did all Americans benefit during this 'golden age'?

The First World War

America didn't join in the First World War when it started. Instead, it sold food, weapons and other goods to Britain and her allies. This created many jobs in America and made lots of businesspeople very rich. America eventually joined the war in 1917 on Britain's side, after the German navy had sunk lots of American ships – and they found out that the Germans were secretly scheming to help Mexico invade America! Over 100 000 American soldiers died fighting, but the impact was much greater in countries like France, Germany, Russia and Britain, which had all been exhausted by the war. In these countries, millions of men had been killed and they had lost valuable farmland, railway lines, factories, cattle and so on. Now the USA, not touched by any of the fighting, produced a high percentage of the world's basic goods (see **Source B**). Skilled inventors and businessmen were now able to exploit these resources and make fortunes from them.

▼ **Source A** *An illustration of a famous American recruitment poster. It is based on a British poster – notice the way the finger and the eyes follow you around as you look at it from different angles.*

▼ **Source B** *By 1920, America was one of the world's leading producers and suppliers of raw materials. This chart shows the percentage of the world's resources made in the USA.*

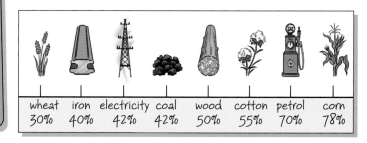

wheat	iron	electricity	coal	wood	cotton	petrol	corn
30%	40%	42%	42%	50%	55%	70%	78%

New things to buy

In 1916, only 15% of American homes had electricity – but nearly 70% of homes had it by 1927. This meant that workers could spend their hard-earned money on any number of ultra-modern electric-powered 'gadgets' which had recently been invented – vacuum cleaners, gramophones (ask your teacher!), toasters, washing machines, radios, telephones, refrigerators, irons, ovens and much more. Huge demand for these goods created jobs in the factories that made them.

▼ **Source C** *An advert for an electric water heater, 1921.*

New ways to make things

American businesspeople, like Henry Ford, were very quick to see the advantages of using the very latest technology to produce goods. He made huge numbers of cars, built bit by bit, pulled along on an **assembly line**, in a massive high-tech factory in Detroit. Glass, steel, rubber and leather went in one end of his factory – cars came out of the other, one every <u>ten</u> seconds! Many **consumer goods** – radios, telephones and ovens – were produced like this. And all the time, as companies got better and quicker at making them, the cheaper the goods became. The more products that people bought, the more jobs were created.

▼ **Source D** *The growth in sales of consumer goods during the 1920s. Amazingly, by 1929, America made nearly 50% of all the world's consumer goods.*

Cars
1919 – 9 million
1929 – 26 million

Telephones
1919 – 10 million
1929 – 20 million

Radios
1919 – 60 000
1929 – 10 million

Refrigerators
For every refrigerator in 1921, there were 167 by 1929.

WISE UP WORDS

- consumer goods   billboards   assembly line
  import duties   tariffs

New ways to buy and sell

The desire to own these new consumer goods was increased by fantastic advertising campaigns. Colourful **billboards**, newspapers and magazines urged people to buy the latest gadget and keep up with their neighbours. Department stores sold the goods on every high street and, for those who didn't live near a large enough town, there was the latest catalogue, full of goods to choose from, which could be delivered to your door. In one famous catalogue, you could buy anything from a tractor to a coffee cup, to a pair of pants! Cinemas and radios carried advertisements too, even encouraging people to take advantage of new 'buy now, pay later' schemes, which meant buyers could pay for goods in small instalments over a fixed period of time. Six out of ten cars were bought this way.

▼ **Source E** *Companies like Coca-Cola made millions because they spent money on advertising slogans, like 'the pause that refreshes'.*

FACT *Buy, buy, buy*

A selection of consumer goods available to buy in 1925.

Help from the government

To help American businesses, the government put high taxes (**import duties** or **tariffs**) on foreign goods entering the country, making foreign-produced goods more expensive. So when faced with the choice of an expensive foreign car or handbag – or a cheaper American-made one – customers would usually choose the one produced in their own country. The government also cut taxes paid by rich people and companies – they wanted rich people to have as much money as possible so they could start more companies and create more jobs!

▼ **Source F** *From an American news article, 1927. Have you ever bought something solely as a result of an advertisement?*

"Advertising makes people want things they didn't even know they wanted. It changes our habits and our way of life, affects what we wear, what we eat and how we pay."

FACT *'You've got bata, hella, bety … bad breath!'*

In 1921, the company that made Listerine Mouthwash used the rather serious-sounding medical word *halitosis* in an advertisement for their product, instead of the more commonly used phrase *bad breath*. This was clearly designed to make people worry that they had a serious medical condition … it worked! Within five years, sales rose from 100 000 bottles to four million bottles a year.

A good time for all?

Not everyone enjoyed the high wages and fantastic job opportunities of the 1920s. In fact, by 1928, half the population were living below the poverty line, not able to afford basics such as food or clothing. They included:

- Farmers – new high-tech machinery like combine harvesters meant they produced more food than ever before. There was more food available than the population could eat so it remained unsold. Farmers who couldn't sell food made little money and were either evicted from their land or forced to sell up. Cotton and wool farmers suffered too. New artificial fibres, such as rayon, were being used instead of natural fibres to make clothing. Cotton and wool factory workers suffered too because there was less demand for their products. 600 000 farmers lost their farms in 1924 alone! All their farm workers would lose their jobs too of course.

- Black workers – thousands of Black Americans worked on farms in the south. As farms closed, they lost their jobs. Many made their way to the cities to find work but could only find low paid jobs – and some factories operated an all-white policy!

- Coal miners – coal mines began to close as oil, gas and electricity were increasingly used as alternatives to heat homes and cook food.

Source G *A poor family of farm workers. What signs are there in the photograph that this family is poor?*

WORK

1. **a** The 1920s are often called 'the boom times' by historians. What do you think the phrase 'boom time' means?

   b Here are seven reasons why there was a 'boom time' in America in the 1920s. Explain how each one helped to cause the economic boom.

   i) the First World War ii) new consumer goods iii) the assembly line iv) advertising v) 'buy now, pay later' schemes vi) import duties vii) low taxes

2. Look at **Source D**. This diagram shows a range of new consumer goods available for Americans to buy in the 1920s. For each one, explain how it would have changed a consumer's life.

3. Did all Americans enjoy the boom times? Give examples in your answer.

GCSE Question time

- Why was there an economic boom in the USA in the 1920s?

- Explain why American farmers faced problems in the 1920s.

Why was Henry Ford so famous?

🎯 AIMS ....

Over the next four pages, you should learn:

- how Henry Ford revolutionised the motor car industry;
- how the production of cheap, reliable motor cars changed the face of America.

Henry Ford built his first car in a rented shed. Banks had refused to lend him any money because they thought his dreams of making a cheap, reliable car were unrealistic! Twenty-five years later, he was the richest man in America and more famous than most presidents. He was earning over $25 000 A DAY and his factory was producing a car every ten seconds!

So how did Ford do it? How could he make cars so quickly … and so well? And how did the car industry, more than any other, help to make America rich in the 1920s?

Henry Ford came from a farming family. His father was an Irish immigrant and his mother was from Holland. His parents wanted their son to be a farmer too but Henry had other plans … and he was far too busy making tools and strange machines from old farm equipment to worry about the family business.

In 1896, he made his first petrol-driven car after reading about one in a science magazine. Seven

1 An electric conveyor belt carried the partly assembled car past the workers who stood in the same spot and did the same job, for example, fitting a wheel or a door over and over again.

2 The tools and equipment the workers needed were brought to them so they didn't waste time fetching things. One man would only be responsible for one or two small jobs. Ford himself said, 'the key is to keep everything moving. Take the work to the man and not the man to the work.'

years later, after raising money by winning car races, he set up his own firm – the Henry Ford Motor Company. He was soon making hundreds of cars but was frustrated by the length of time it took to make each one. He realised that if he wanted to make lots more money, he needed to make them faster AND cheaper. By 1911, he came up with a solution – the assembly line.

> ## WISE UP WORD
> • mass production

So how does an assembly line work?

▼ *Before the assembly line, cars stayed in one place whilst workers wasted time and energy walking about, getting tools and carrying pieces of equipment to the car. One car could take nearly two days to build.*

▼ **Source A**   *Henry Ford, 1922.*

"In the chassis [frame of car] assembly line, there are 45 separate operations … some men do only two small operations, others do more. The man who places the part doesn't fasten it. The man who puts the bolt in doesn't put the nut on. The man who puts the nut on doesn't tighten it. On operation number 34, the car gets its petrol … on operation number 44, the radiator is filled with water and on operation number 45 the car drives onto the road."

3 For many years, Ford made just one type of car – The Model T or 'Tin Lizzie' as it was nicknamed. It was **mass-produced**. Costs were kept low because there was just one engine size, one colour available (black – Ford didn't want workers wasting time changing the paint in spray guns!), no side windows, no speedometer and no windscreen wipers.

4 As Ford's factory got quicker, the price of the car got lower. Costing nearly $800 in 1911, the price in 1928 was only $295. As a result, 15 million people bought Model Ts between 1911 and 1929! By the time production stopped and Ford changed to different models, there were six Tin Lizzies driving out of his Detroit factory every minute!

▼ **Source B** *The Ford assembly line, 1928.*

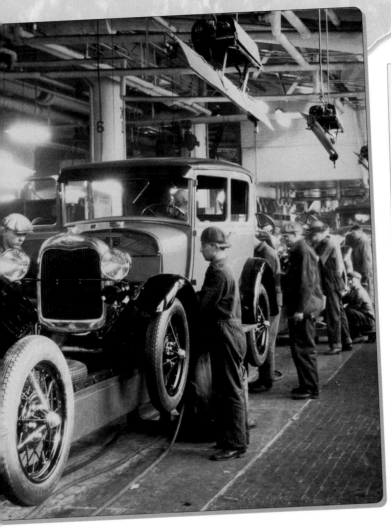

▼ **Source C** *This source describes the economic impact of the car. There were three big car producers in all – Ford, Chrysler and General Motors – but Ford was by far the biggest.*

"Car-making used up 20% of America's steel, 80% of her rubber, 75% of her plate glass and 65% of her leather. The more cars made, the more jobs there were in these industries. Cars on the road used seven billion gallons of petrol a year and this made the oil producers of Texas rich. New roads had to be built … and this meant jobs in the construction industry. And along the new roads sprung up thousands of garages, 'gas stations', restaurants, 'motels', hot dog stands – all providing even more jobs."

▼ **Source D** *Model Ts on a high street, 1926. By 1928, one in five people owned at least one car. It has been estimated that by this time, Henry Ford was earning $25 000 a day – that's over £2 million today!*

Henry Ford was a brilliant businessman and a mechanical genius. His Model T – 'an affordable car for ordinary people' as he called it – changed the motor industry forever. Despite it being slow, ugly and difficult to drive, it was sturdy, very reliable and built with easy-to-change parts – and it just kept getting cheaper and cheaper to buy! It was the right product at just the right time. It caught the public's imagination when they were desperate for new gadgets and a chance to see what was beyond their own backyards.

By 1926, there were nearly 20 million cars on America's roads – and one out of every two was a Model T Ford. Look carefully at **Sources C** to **I** – they give you an idea of the impact of the motor car and, in particular, the Henry Ford Motor Company.

▼ **Source E** *Ford's influence, written by a modern historian.*

"Ford's ideas on the assembly line and mass production were copied across America. Soon, all sorts of products — like radios, telephones and even tin cans — were mass produced on the assembly line."

▼ **Source F** *Calvin Coolidge, President of the USA 1922–1928.*

"The business of America is business … the man who builds a factory builds a temple. The man who works there worships there."

▼ **Source G** *An American housewife, quoted in Middletown in Transition.*

"We'd rather go without clothes than give up our car. I never feel as close to my family as I do when we are together in the car."

▼ **Source H** *A photograph of Henry Ford with his son, Edsel. Ford gave huge amounts of money to charity – helping schools, museums and orphanages – but hated Jews and used his own newspaper to launch attacks on them. He banned trade unions in his factory and used 'bully boys' to beat up any men who complained too loudly about their jobs.*

American society itself began to change as more and more people bought cars. Some changes were negative – like traffic jams, road accidents and pollution – but others were for the better. Car owners felt a new sense of freedom because they could go wherever they wanted, whenever they chose.

▼ **Source I** *Some criticisms of the motor car. Ask your teacher what 'courting' means!*

"Critics of the motor car said that the assembly line made workers into unskilled slaves, doing boring and unrewarding work. Some critics also pointed to the fact that gangsters were able to use 'getaway cars' to escape justice. They also called the car 'a house of prostitution on wheels' because it became common for lovers to do their courting on car back seats."

WORK

1   **a** In no more than 50 words, describe how Ford's assembly line worked. You should draw a diagram to go with your explanation.

   b In what ways was the assembly line an improvement on previous methods of making cars?

   c Why could Ford constantly reduce the price of his cars but still manage to make huge profits?

2   Make two lists. Firstly, list all the advantages of owning a car. Secondly, list all the disadvantages or problems created by cars.

3   An obituary is a piece of writing about someone who has just died. They appear in newspapers. Henry Ford died in 1947. You must include information about his family, his early career, the impact of the assembly line and his motor cars. The first part has been done for you:

Henry Ford – motor millionaire

Born: 1864 in Detroit

Family: Son of Irish immigrant father and…

GCSE Question time

- Why was Henry Ford so important to American industry in the 1920s?

'Blood on the leaves'

AIMS ....

After completing the work on these two pages, test your understanding by making sure you can:
- explain what 'Jim Crow Laws' were;
- identify how some black people were treated during the 1920s.

Source A

Look at **Source A**. These two black men, Abram Smith and Thomas Shipp, have just been dragged from the local jail by a mob of 5000 angry locals in Marion, Indiana. They were accused of killing a white man but no trial ever took place – they were hanged – or **lynched** – long before that could happen! This famous photograph from the 1920s is said to have inspired singing superstar Billie Holiday to write the hit song 'Strange Fruit' (see **Source B**).

Source B *'Strange Fruit' by Billie Holiday.*

"Southern trees bear strange fruit,
Blood on the leaves and blood at the root,
Black bodies swinging in the southern
    breeze,
Strange fruit hanging from the poplar
    trees.

Pastoral scene of the gallant south,
The bulging eyes and the twisted mouth,
Scent of magnolias, sweet and fresh,
Then the sudden smell of burning flesh.

Here is fruit for the crows to pluck,
For the rain to gather, for the wind to
    suck,
For the sun to rot, for the trees to
    drop,
Here is a strange and bitter crop."

Lynchings, like the one pictured in **Source A**, had been taking place in America for many years. 123 black people were lynched in 1897, 84 in 1903 and 61 in 1921. On most occasions, the police made no effort to stop it happening. Many of the victims were probably innocent of any crime, but justice wasn't really the purpose of this terror – it was to remind Black Americans that the White Americans were firmly in control … and they intended to keep it that way.

WISE UP WORDS
- lynching   segregation

Although free – slavery had ended in America in 1865 – many black people faced the threat of violence, intimidation and racial discrimination on an almost daily basis. Many states, especially those in the south where the black population was highest, tried to keep control over black people by passing laws to keep them completely separate or **segregated**. These 'Jim Crow Laws' ('Jim Crow' was an insulting name for a black person) covered all aspects of life. Black Americans were stopped from using the same restaurants, hotels, cinemas, racetracks, swimming pools, libraries, taxis and even cemeteries as white people. The American Red Cross even kept black people's blood donations separate in their blood banks! Ways were even found to stop black people voting, like making them pass a difficult literacy test or forcing them to pay high taxes before they voted (which most couldn't afford to pay, of course).

▾ **Source C** *'Jim Crow Laws' in action. A segregated drinking fountain.*

Nearly two million (out of 12 million) Black Americans left the southern states where the lynchings took place and where racial discrimination was at its strongest, and headed north. There were more jobs in the new industries in the northern states … and no 'Jim Crow Laws'. However, there was still racism. Black people were usually the last to be given jobs and were the first to be fired. They occupied the worst housing in the poorest cities. Some factories only employed white workers or paid their black workers the lowest wages. Even so, the opportunities for black people appeared to be greater in the north and more and more moved there every year. Indeed, by the 1920s, the black population of both Chicago and New York had more than doubled since 1900.

FACT *NAACP*

In 1910, WEB DuBois – the great grandson of an African slave – set up the NAACP, the National Association for the Advancement of Coloured People. They worked hard to improve the rights of black people, such as the right to vote, but the politicians of the 1920s failed to introduce any of their suggestions. The NAACP still exists today and has attracted support from world famous pop stars, film stars and sportspeople.

FACT *Back to Africa?*

Some Africans supported the idea of returning to Africa – the place where they had originally lived before being taken to America as slaves. Marcus Garvey became the leader of the 'Back to Africa' campaign and is well known for first using the famous phrase 'Black is beautiful' – a statement of pride and self-respect. However, the whole movement failed after Garvey was jailed for fraud.

WORK

1 Test your understanding of this double page by writing a sentence or two about the following:
   • lynching • Jim Crow Laws • NAACP
   • 'Back to Africa'

2 Look at **Sources A** and **B**.
   a Explain how the photograph might have inspired Billie Holiday to write 'Strange Fruit'.
   b No one was ever prosecuted for the murders of Abram Smith and Thomas Shipp. Suggest reasons why people were able to get away with such a violent crime.

3 a Why did many Black Americans choose to leave the southern states and travel to northern states?
   b In what ways did Black Americans still suffer discrimination in the north?

Who were the Ku Klux Klan?

One of America's most racist terror groups was a secret society known as the Ku Klux Klan or KKK. Between 1920 and 1925, around five million white Americans joined the KKK. The KKK's main aim was to maintain white **supremacy** over black people and immigrants and 'keep them in their place'.

Dressed in white sheets, white hoods and carrying American flags, their methods of violence and intimidation included whipping, branding with acid, kidnapping, castration and lynching. They stripped some of their victims and put burning hot tar and feathers on their bodies (see **Source A**).

Led by a dentist from Texas called Hiram Wesley Evans, the KKK was strongest in the southern states where there was a large black population. However, Evans – or the 'Imperial Wizard' as he was known – controlled local units or dens of Klansmen all over America. New members joined through secret, elaborate ceremonies that involved American flags, burning crosses, hooded faces and secret code-words known as **klonversations** (see **Source B**). They even had a strict rule book known as the 'Kloran'.

Most of the members were poor white people who were afraid of black people and immigrant workers because they were prepared to work for low wages. But the KKK also had members who were policemen, judges, teachers and politicians. Fortunately, the mass appeal of the KKK did not last long. In 1925, a popular local Klan leader named David Stephenson was convicted of the brutal kidnapping, rape and murder of a young woman. At his trial, he exposed many of the secrets of the KKK. He was sentenced to life imprisonment and within a year, KKK membership had fallen from five million to 300 000.

▼ **Source A** *A new member swears an oath of loyalty to the KKK whilst a young black man is tarred and feathered. This picture is based on an event that took place in Texas in 1923.*

WISE UP WORDS
- supremacy   klonversations

▼ **Source B** *KKK secret codes. Why did they need, or want, a secret language?*

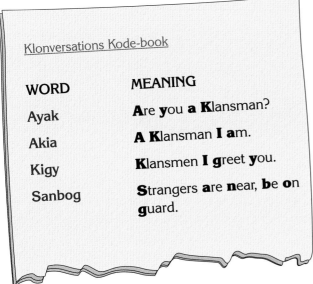

Klonversations Kode-book

WORD	MEANING
Ayak	**A**re **y**ou **a K**lansman?
Akia	**A K**lansman **I a**m.
Kigy	**K**lansmen **I g**reet **y**ou.
Sanbog	**S**trangers **a**re **n**ear, **b**e **o**n **g**uard.

▼ **Source C** *These acts of violence were carried out by the KKK in Alabama in the 1920s. Members believed that the most superior American citizens were white Anglo-Saxon Protestants (WASPs), like the ones who first settled in America in the 1600s. As a result, Jews and Catholics were also on the 'hate list' because the KKK saw themselves as 'defenders' of their Protestant religion.*

"A lad was whipped with branches until his back was ribboned flesh; a black woman was beaten and left to catch pneumonia and die; a white girl, a divorcee, was beaten until she was unconscious; an immigrant was flogged until his back was a pulp because he married an American woman; a black man was whipped until he sold his land to a white woman for a fraction of its value."

▼ **Source D** *The Ku Klux Klan is still active in parts of America today.*

WORK

1 Look at **Source A**.
  a In your own words, describe exactly what is going on in the picture.
  b Suggest two reasons why the Klan members wore white hoods.

2 a Using the sources to help you, describe the sort of person who might have joined the KKK in the 1920s.
  b Why do you think members of the KKK were able to get away with such violence without being punished?
  c Why did KKK membership start to fall after 1925?

3 Look at **Source C**. Five people are beaten and/or whipped in this source. Suggest reasons why any two of them were attacked.

GCSE Question time
• What discrimination did Black Americans suffer during the 1920s?

What was a flapper?

AIMS ....

After studying these two pages, you need to be able to give:

- an explanation of what a flapper was;
- examples of what flappers did;
- reasons why more women became more independent in the 1920s.

▲ *Source A*

Look at **Source A**. The two young women in the photograph are **flappers**. They have just been arrested on a beach in Chicago for being 'indecently dressed'. To put it simply, their swimming costumes are just too revealing for the 1920s – they have shown too much flesh and have shocked an onlooker into calling the police!

Flappers, the fashionable, independent young women of the 1920s, rebelled against the way women had been treated for many years. They hated the fact that men had the best jobs and earned the most money. They rebelled against the sort of clothes that women were traditionally expected to wear (see **Source B**) and detested the role that many men assumed that women should take – the role of wife and mother.

During the First World War, millions of women had taken over jobs that had been previously done by men. They not only did the work as well as men, but the money they earned gave them a sense of independence – they no longer had to rely on their husband's wealth!

After the war, women found jobs in many of the new factories and offices that opened during the boom years. In 1920, American women were given the right to vote. Most historians agree that this new freedom was the spark that started the 'flapper phenomenon'.

A flapper would be easy to recognise. They had short, bobbed hairstyles and wore lots of make-up. They dressed in short skirts, revealing tops and wore silk stockings rolled to just above the knee. They smoked cigarettes and drank alcohol in public. Some rode motorbikes and went to nightclubs with men without a **chaperone**. They held their dance partners close without wearing gloves and some of them even had sex before marriage. Some worried Americans even formed an **Anti-Flirt League** to protest against their behaviour.

A survey in 1900 showed that nearly 80% of college students questioned had not had sex before marriage. A similar survey in 1920 found that only 31% had not had sex before marriage. Times were definitely changing!

▼ **Source B** *A woman*

long hair, tied up under a hat

pale skin, little make-up

tight corset that pulled in the waist

long sleeves, covering the arms

long dress, covering legs

▼ **Source C** *A flapper of the 1920s. They were mainly middle-class and upper-class women from the northern states of America. They earned their own money and rebelled against their restricted lives, but for many poorer women, and those in the more traditional southern states, life went on as it had done for many years.*

- short hair
- cocktail
- Chanel No. 5 perfume
- suntan and make-up
- bangles and long beads
- low waist
- high hemline
- cigarette
- flesh-coloured stockings

▼ **Source D** *The president of Florida University, 1923. Many older people saw flappers as an example of the evils of modern life. These people felt that family life, religion and traditional values were threatened by their new freedom.*

"The low-cut dresses, the stockings and short skirts are born of the devil and are carrying the present and future generations of this country to destruction."

▶ **Source E** *Two flappers bravely dancing the Charleston on the roof of a Chicago hotel in 1926. The Charleston, like the One Step, the Black Bottom and the Tango, were favourite dances in the 1920s. As jazz music swept the nation on radios and in nightclubs, these high-energy dances were a welcome relief to the old ballroom dancing and waltzes of America before the war.*

▼ **Source F** *A flapper interviewed for a magazine in the 1920s. The name 'flapper' comes from the fact that some of these young women didn't bother to tie their laces on the long boots they often wore. Instead, they let them 'flap' around their ankles.*

"'Do nice girls do it?' a girl was asked. 'Well', she said, 'I don't really want to be kissed by some of the fellows I know, but I let them do it anyway, rather than let them think I wouldn't dare!'"

WISE UP WORDS

- chaperone   flappers   Anti-Flirt League

WORK

1 Look at **Source A**.
   a Explain why these two women have been arrested.
   b Do you think anything about their behaviour whilst they were being taken away has shocked onlookers?
2 In your opinion, what gave some women a new sense of freedom during the 1910s and 1920s?
3 Imagine you are one of many thousands of Americans who joined the Anti-Flirt League in the 1920s. Write a letter to your friend, who has no knowledge of flappers, explaining what they are and how disgusted you are with them. You might also explain the role of the League. Use **Sources A** to **F** to help you to write your 'angry' letter.

GCSE Question time

- Explain why the lives of some women changed in the 1920s.

What shall we do today?

AIMS ....

After studying the next six pages, you should be able to identify:
- at least five popular leisure activities in the 1920s;
- reasons why the movie industry boomed.

For many, the 1920s was a period in American history when people were having lots of fun, enjoying loud music, wild parties and new forms of entertainment. Millions of people had more money and more leisure time than ever before. As you must realise, not everyone enjoyed this 'wild ride', but enough did to earn the decade a world famous nickname – the 'Roaring Twenties'.

Wonderful nonsense

The Roaring Twenties was a time of **crazes**. Millions became hooked on a complicated Chinese board game called mah-jong before crosswords became all the rage. When the crossword craze died out, marathon dancing and flagpole sitting became popular. People would see how long they could dance without stopping or how long they could sit on top of a flagpole without falling off. Alvin 'Shipwreck' Kelly set the record when he remained on top of a flagpole for 49 days!

▶ **Source A** *A marathon dancing competition, 1928. Alma Cummings was American champion. Using many different partners, she managed to dance for 27 hours in 1923.*

Sport

The 1920s were a golden age for American sport. For the first time, sportspeople became sports *stars* with celebrity status. Babe Ruth of baseball's New York Yankees became a national hero after setting a home run record – 60 in the 1927 season – which lasted until 1961. By 1930, he was earning $80 000 a year, the equivalent of nearly £7 million a year today. Bobby Jones took the golfing world by storm – he won the British Open in 1926, 1927 and 1930 and the US Open in 1923, 1926, 1929 and 1930.

Radio broadcasts, newspapers and magazines helped bring major sports events to a mass audience. Around 60 million radio listeners heard the 1927 World Heavyweight Boxing title fight between Jack Dempsey and Gene Tunney.

▼ **Source B** *Baseball legend Babe Ruth pictured with the world's largest baseball in 1927.*

New music

Jazz was the most popular music of the 1920s. For the first time, whites were exposed to black music – and millions loved it! This new sound, originating in the black neighbourhood of Harlem, New York, provided great opportunities for black musicians such as Louis Armstrong, Duke Ellington, Bessie Smith, Fats Waller and Benny Goodman. They made big money from nightclub and radio performances, and record sales.

▼ **Source C** *A popular jazz musician speaking in the 1920s. Even today, the 1920s are known as the Jazz Age.*

"Music is entering more and more into the daily lives of people. The Negro musicians of America are playing a great part in this change. They are not held back by traditions. They have new ideas and constantly experiment. They are causing new blood to flow into the veins of music. The jazz players make their instruments do entirely new things, things trained musicians are taught to avoid…. Jazz has come to stay because it is an expression of the times – the breathless, energetic, super active times in which we are living."

▼ **Source E** *Some criticisms of jazz music from the 1920s. These comments only made jazz more popular with young Americans.*

- Jazz music causes drunkenness. All sense is lost and animal passions take over in its presence.

- Jazz lyrics, written in Negro brothels, are an offence to women.

- Jazz has a demoralising effect on the human brain, which has been demonstrated by scientists. Jazz stimulates people to do extreme deeds; it is harmful and dangerous.

▶ **Source D** *A poster advertising a performance by Louis Armstrong and his band. Ironically, many of the clubs in which the country's most famous jazz performers worked had an 'all-white' policy – the only black people allowed in were the musicians! Even Harlem's legendary Cotton Club was run and owned by white people.*

Lucky Lindy

Perhaps the most famous 1920s American of all was the pilot Charles A Lindbergh. In May 1927, he became the first man to do what many Americans had died trying to do for many years – he flew non-stop across the Atlantic Ocean from New York to Paris. In his plane *Spirit of St Louis*, he had taken five sandwiches, two pints of water and an inflatable boat. He took no map and no parachute!

After a 33½-hour flight, which had seen Lindbergh slap himself for hours on end to keep awake, he touched down in Paris and immediately became a superstar. Within a week, he had received over half a million 'well done' letters and was well on his way to becoming one of America's greatest ever heroes. At one point, he was so famous that he couldn't send his clothes to the dry-cleaners because the staff kept them as souvenirs! In 1932, the whole country mourned when his baby son was kidnapped and brutally murdered. Even today, there aren't many American towns or cities without a Lindbergh Avenue or Charles Lindbergh Boulevard.

▼ **Source F** *Before his flight, some reporters had called Lindbergh 'a flying fool'. He is pictured here with his mum.*

The movies

One of the biggest success stories of the 1920s was the movie industry. Hollywood, just outside the Californian city of Los Angeles, enjoyed year round sunshine and many of the big movie companies – MGM, Warner Brothers and Paramount – had their studios there. Movies were already big business before the 1920s, with weekly audiences of 35 million in 1919 but, during the next decade, audiences nearly trebled to a high of 100 million people a WEEK going to the movies to watch films in 1930. That's as many as go to visit the cinema in a year in Britain today. Part of the success of the movie industry was something called the **star system**.

◀ *Source G A film poster for a famous Charlie Chaplin comedy. By the time this movie was made, English-born Chaplin was earning about $1500 a week, a fortune during the 1920s. Aged 28, Chaplin signed Hollywood's first ever $1 million contract.*

The star system was a term used to describe the way movie studios promoted their stars, not just the films they were in. They made sure that the media had full access to the star, making them do magazine interviews, photo shoots, radio shows and public appearances. The stars, often presented as sex symbols, attracted obsessive fans (see **Source H**). Also, people were attracted to their lifestyles, copying the way their favourite star mixed their cocktails, ate their dinner, styled their hair and wore their clothes. Film-makers even realised that the star of a film was often more important than its plot – people would pay to see the film even if it was terrible! As a result of the star system,

performers like Charlie Chaplin, Rudolf Valentino, Clara Bow, Douglas Fairbanks and Laurel and Hardy became household names. By 1929, Hollywood film studios were making over 500 films a year, giving employment to thousands and entertainment to millions who flocked to see comedies, romances, adventure stories and historical epics. By the 1930s, Hollywood stars even had to compete with cartoon characters when Walt Disney brought Mickey Mouse, Pluto, Donald Duck and Goofy to life.

Until 1927, all movies were silent. Words appeared on screen at regular intervals and a piano player provided background music. Then *The Jazz Singer* was released, the first 'talking film', or 'talkie' as they were known. This boosted cinema audience figures to an all-time high because moviegoers were desperate to see how their favourite movie star spoke. In fact, 'talkies' ruined the careers of many actors and actresses who looked great … but had strange voices or funny accents!

▼ *Source H Rudolph Valentino, pictured here with actress Vilma Banky in* The Son of the Sheik, *1926. This was his last film; he died aged 31, soon after filming finished. A crowd of over 100 000 queued for miles to see the body in its coffin and dozens were injured when a fight broke out amongst the mourners over who loved him the most!*

▾ **Source I** The Jazz Singer, *playing at Warners' Theatre, New York, soon after opening in 1927.*

▾ **Source J** *The movies horrified many older Americans. They worried about the sexual content of some films. When 36 states threatened to ban several films, Hollywood introduced its own code of conduct – the Hays Code – to censor their film industry.*

THE HAYS CODE

· No kiss should last longer than seven feet of film [about 3 seconds].

· Members of the clergy should not be used as comic characters or villains.

· Nudity is forbidden.

· No film character should ever profit from safe-cracking, arson or murder. Acts like this should not be shown in detail in case moviegoers copy them.

Signed MGM, Paramount, Warner Brothers, United Artists

WISE UP WORDS

● star system   crazes   jazz

FACT   *More time, more money*

During the 1920s, the average working week for a typical American dropped from 47.4 to 44.2 hours. Average wages rose by 11%. To put it simply, people had more leisure time and more money to spend on it!

WORK

1 **a** Explain what is meant by the word 'craze'. Use a modern-day example of a 'craze' in your answer.

   b Describe three crazes from the 1920s.

2 Babe Ruth and Bobby Jones were two of the world's first sports celebrities. What do we mean by the term sports celebrity?

3 Look at **Source E**.

   a For what reasons did the writer dislike jazz music?

   b Why do you think criticism of jazz music made many young people want to listen to it even more?

   c Can you think of any other reason, linked to race, why many Americans objected to jazz music?

4 **a** Do you think 'Lucky Lindy' and 'the flying fool' were appropriate nicknames for Charles Lindbergh? Explain your answer.

   b Why do you think Lindbergh was so popular?

5 **a** Make a list of reasons why the movie industry and movie stars were so popular in the 1920s.

   b Why is *The Jazz Singer* such an important film?

   c What was the Hays Code and why do you think it was needed?

6 Draw a diagram or create a poster that summarises the main features of entertainment and popular culture in the Roaring Twenties. Use the text on pages 26–31 to help you.

GCSE Question time

● What were the main features of the 'Roaring Twenties'?

● Describe the cinema industry in the USA during the 1920s.

What was Prohibition ... and why did it fail?

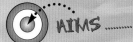

AIMS ....

After these four pages, you should be able to:

- Write at least one sentence about each of the Wise Up Words on page 34;
- list the reasons why Prohibition was introduced in the 1920s and why it failed.

At midnight on 16 January 1920, America introduced a new law. Seconds later, millions of people were breaking it. They would continue to break it until the law was **repealed** (ended) in 1933. Most of the lawbreakers would never get punished.

Some historians say that America's newest law was one of the country's biggest ever mistakes. So what law were people so keen to break? How did they break it? And why was it introduced in the first place?

Prohibition, as the new law was known, prohibited any American from selling, making or carrying around any drink containing more than 0.5% alcohol (most beers, for example, contain 5% alcohol). The ban on booze wasn't a sudden thing. For many years there had been a strong campaign against alcohol, led by pressure groups like the **Anti-Saloon League** (see **Source A**). Many Americans supported a ban, claiming that the 'demon drink' damaged family life and caused idleness, sickness and debt.

▸ **Source A** *A 1919 leaflet published by the Anti-Saloon League, a religious organisation that wanted to ban alcoholic drink everywhere in America. In total, the ASL printed over one hundred million of these leaflets! The First World War even helped the ASL. They claimed that any American who drank beer was a traitor to their country because many of the beers on sale in America were made in Germany or by German immigrants who had settled in America!*

SLAVES OF THE SALOON

The saloon business cannot exist without slaves. You may smile at that statement, but it is absolutely true. Is not the man who is addicted to the drink habit a slave? There are 1,000,000 such slaves in the United States. They are slaves of the saloon. They go out and work a week or a month, draw their pay, go into the saloon, and hand the saloon keeper their money for something which ruins their own lives. Is not this slavery? Has there ever been in the history of the world a worse system of slavery? It is quite natural, of course, that the slaveholder should not care to liberate these slaves.— *Richmond P. Hobson.*

A woman entered a barroom, and advanced quietly to her husband, who sat drinking with three other men. "Thinkin' ye'd be too busy to come home to supper, Jack, I've fetched it to you here." And she departed. The man laughed awkwardly. He invited his friends to share the meal with him. Then he removed the cover from the dish. The dish was empty. It contained a slip of paper that said: "I hope you will enjoy your supper. It is the same your wife and children have at home."— *Chicago Chronicle.*

The liquor traffic, like the slave trade or piracy, cannot be mended, and therefore must be actually ended.— *Joseph Cook.*

▼ **Source B** *From an American school textbook in the 1920s.*

> "A cat or dog can be killed if it drinks a small glass of beer. A boy once drank whiskey from a flask he had found and died the next day."

FACT *The law*

Prohibition is actually a nickname. Officially, the ban on alcohol is the 18th Amendment (change) to the United States Constitution. The Amendment states that '...the manufacture, sale or transportation of intoxicating liquors ... within the United States ... for beverage purposes is hereby prohibited.' Interestingly, it was never illegal to buy or drink it! The **Volstead Act** later set down penalties for breaking the new law and defined 'intoxicating liquor' as any drink that contained more than 0.5% of alcohol.

▼ **Source C** *Some of the many million litres of alcohol poured down the drain when America went 'dry'.*

WORK

1 Look at **Source A**.
   a For what reasons, according to this poster, did the Anti-Saloon League want to ban alcohol?
   b '**Source A** is of no value to a historian because it is so biased.' Do you agree with this statement? Explain your answer carefully.
2 Look at **Source B**. Was this written by a supporter or an opponent of Prohibition? Give reasons for your answer.
3 Why was Prohibition introduced? Make a list, giving as many reasons as you can find on these two pages.

Prohibition never worked. The reason for this was quite simple – people still wanted to drink. They were prepared to break a law they never wanted ... and criminal gangs were only too willing to get the alcohol for them. These gangs ran illegal bars called **speakeasies**, which sold **bootleg** alcohol smuggled in from abroad by **bootleggers**. They also sold **moonshine** – a home-made spirit that was sometimes so strong it caused serious illness. In fact, deaths from alcohol poisoning went up from 98 in 1920 to nearly 800 in 1926! Speakeasies were hidden away in cellars or private hotel rooms and drinkers had to give passwords or knock on the door in code to gain entry.

▼ **Source D** *Advertising an illegal speakeasy in a newspaper or magazine was against the law. Instead, signs and directions were chalked onto the pavement to show the way.*

▼ **Source E** *Inside a speakeasy, 1925. One club, The Hunt Club in New York, had 23 000 members.*

A few years after the introduction of Prohibition, criminal gangs were making millions from bootlegging and speakeasies. They made so much money that they could bribe police, lawyers and judges to cooperate with them and not prosecute. They also made money through fixing horse and dog racing, running brothels and **racketeering**. This was when businessmen and shopkeepers paid money to the gangs to stop them smashing up their premises. One gang leader, the famous Al Capone, made $10 million a year from racketeering. Other gang leaders, or **gangsters**, as they were known, included Dutch Schultz, 'Bugs' Moran, 'Lucky' Luciano, 'Machine Gun' Kelly and Vito 'Chicken Head' Gurino! These men settled their business rivalries in gunfights and bomb attacks, which led to a new phrase being used in America – **organised crime**.

By the 1930s, it was clear that Prohibition was just not working – there were now approximately 200 000 speakeasies in America! In New York alone, there were 32 000 speakeasies, yet there were only 15 000 bars *before* Prohibition – it seemed that the law to ban booze was making it more popular than ever!

WISE UP WORDS

- Prohibition   Anti-Saloon League   Volstead Act   speakeasies   bootleg   bootlegger   moonshine   racketeering   organised crime   gangster   repeal

By 1933, many realised that the Prohibition experiment had failed. The attempt to make America a less violent, more honest and moral country had resulted in the rise of gangsters, organised crime and police corruption! In early 1933, one of new American President Roosevelt's first steps was to repeal Prohibition. Americans could (legally) drink again.

▼ **Source F** *Based on an interview with Elmer Gertz, a Chicago lawyer in the 1920s.*

"You'd go into what seemed like an ordinary restaurant that served fried chicken and spaghetti. The wine would be served in coffee cups so that if the place was raided, you'd appear to be drinking coffee not wine … Prohibition taught Americans to disrespect the law … it taught them that crime could pay."

▼ **Source G** *US police catch a group of bootleggers with crates of illegal alcohol hidden in their car.*

▼ **Source H** *Arrests for drinking offences in Philadelphia, 1920–1925 (figures from the Philadelphia police department).*

Year	Drunk	Drunk and disorderly	Drink driving	Habitual drunkards	TOTAL
1920	14 313	6097	–	33	20 443
1921	21 850	5232	494	33	27 609
1922	36 299	7925	472	50	44 746
1923	45 226	8076	645	177	54 124
1924	47 805	6404	683	874	55 766
1925	51 361	5522	820	814	58 517

FACT *Why do we call it that?*

'Bootlegging' got its name in the 1600s when Britain ruled parts of what is now the USA. The British made people pay taxes on any alcoholic drink so smugglers used to hide booze in their long leather boots to avoid paying any tax. 'Speakeasies' got their name because customers had to speak quietly so that they were not discovered. 'Speak easy please' was what a barman would often say to noisy guests.

WORK

1 Write a sentence or two explaining each of the following words: • speakeasies • bootleggers • moonshine • racketeering

2 Look at **Source F**.
  a How did diners conceal their alcoholic drinks?
  b Does this source suggest that the public supported bootlegging? Explain your answer carefully.
  c According to the source, what was one of the worst consequences of Prohibition?

3 Look at **Source H**. Do these statistics demonstrate that Prohibition was successful? Explain your answer carefully.

4 Make a choice. *Either* • Write a short essay setting out the main reasons why Prohibition failed. Mention: the lack of public support; the problems of law enforcement and police corruption; organised crime and big profits. *Or* • Write a speech that is part of a campaign to end Prohibition. Mention: why people don't support Prohibition; the consequences of Prohibition; the evidence of its failure.

The Al Capone story

AIMS ....

After studying the next four pages, you should be able to identify key events in the life of one of the Prohibition era's most infamous gangsters.

Alphonse 'Scarface' Capone is the most infamous gangster of all time. At the height of his power, he was making $2 million a week through illegal gambling dens, brothels, bootlegging and racketeering. He ran his multi-million dollar empire like a business – and dealt viciously with anyone who dared to get in his way!

But how much do you know about 'Big Al'? What sort of family did he come from? How did he get involved in crime? Why did he have so much power? And for what reasons was he eventually sent to jail?

1 Alphonse Capone was born on 17 January 1899 in Brooklyn, New York.

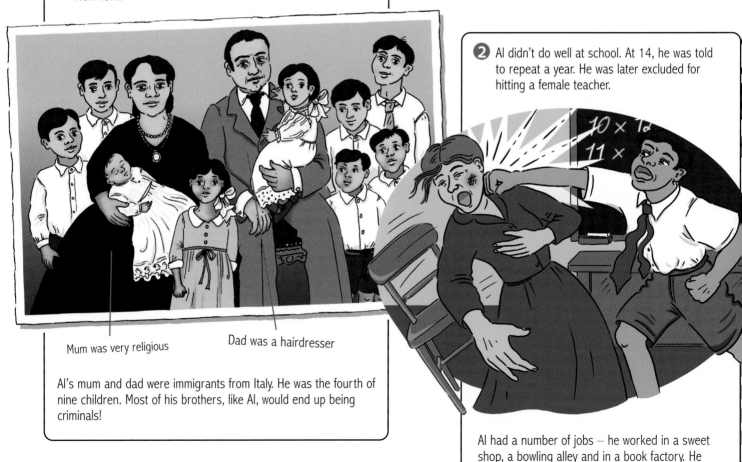

Mum was very religious

Dad was a hairdresser

Al's mum and dad were immigrants from Italy. He was the fourth of nine children. Most of his brothers, like Al, would end up being criminals!

2 Al didn't do well at school. At 14, he was told to repeat a year. He was later excluded for hitting a female teacher.

Al had a number of jobs — he worked in a sweet shop, a bowling alley and in a book factory. He also joined a young street gang called the 'Five Pointers' who terrorised his neighbourhood.

3 At 18, Al got a job as a barman and bouncer. One night he insulted a local tough guy's sister and he slashed Al across the face. Al hated his scar (and his nickname) and often tried to cover it up with make-up. If anyone asked, he said he did it fighting in the war.

'My you've got a beautiful ass. I really mean that!'

'Why you little....!'

Al soon started to get a reputation for being vicious. In 1919, he beat a policeman to death — but nothing was proven.

4 Al left New York in 1919 and moved to Chicago, America's second largest city. A gang boss called Terrible Johnny Torrio had offered him a job.

TORRIO'S FOUR DEUCES

DO THIS, DO THAT.

Yes boss, no problem boss.

I hate taking orders.

Torrio and Al soon took over a few of the other gangs. Chicago was perfect for criminals because many policemen, judges and even the mayor took bribes to 'look the other way'.

5 Torrio and Al were soon making a fortune from bootlegging, protection rackets, fixing horse and dog races and organising prostitutes. Al liked to show off with his money and enjoyed being photographed.

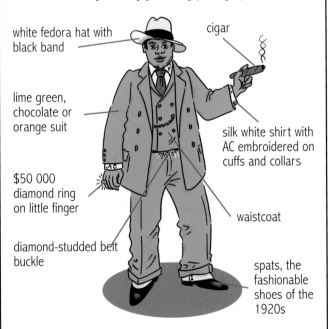

white fedora hat with black band

cigar

lime green, chocolate or orange suit

silk white shirt with AC embroidered on cuffs and collars

$50 000 diamond ring on little finger

waistcoat

diamond-studded belt buckle

spats, the fashionable shoes of the 1920s

Al was arrested from time to time but no witnesses could ever be found!

6 In 1925, Torrio retired (he kept being shot). Al took over, aged 26. Other rival gangs kept trying to kill him so he surrounded himself with bodyguards and drove a bulletproof car capable of 110mph (the average car did 40mph).

steel, armour-plated body

two-centimetre thick bulletproof glass

hinged rear window so he could fire on anyone chasing him

secret rear-gunners compartment

weighed 8000lbs (as heavy as three cars today)

By 1927, Al had 700 men working for him. One by one, his rivals were 'rubbed out' — 227 gangsters killed in four years.

7 On 14 February 1929, Capone attempted to get rid of his biggest rival — 'Bugs' Moran and his North Side Gang.

Dressed as policemen, two of Al's hit men shot dead seven members of the gang in the St Valentine's Day Massacre. Moran survived but soon retired.

9 In 1931, Al was sentenced to 11 years. He was released in 1939, suffering from a brain disease, probably caused by a sexually transmitted infection he picked up from a prostitute in the 1920s.

Al never went back to his gangster lifestyle and retired to Florida. He was so poorly he spent some of his final days fishing in his swimming pool. He died on 25 January 1947 from a massive heart attack.

8 By 1930, Capone had made such a bad name for himself that government FBI agents in Washington vowed to jail him. He was declared Public Enemy Number 1!

No people could ever be found who witnessed any of Al's crimes but he was eventually jailed for not paying his taxes!

▼ **_Source A_** *A statement made by Al Capone. Lake Shore Drive was a rich area of Chicago.*

"I make my money by supplying a popular demand. If I break the law, my customers — who are some of the best people in Chicago — are as guilty as I am. The only difference between us is that I sell and they buy … I call myself a businessman. When I sell liquor, they call it bootlegging — when my customers serve it on a silver tray on Lake Shore Drive, they call it hospitality."

▼ **Source B** *Al Capone in March 1930 on the front cover of* Time, *one of America's biggest-selling weekly magazines. If you look carefully, you can see his scar. Capone achieved celebrity status in America – he was cheered when seen out in public, he opened jazz clubs, organised expensive parties and went to the best sports events. Everyone knew of his activities but it was impossible to convict him for any brutal crimes because of his control of the police.*

March 24, 1930

TIME
The Weekly Newsmagazine

ALPHONSE ("SCARFACE") CAPONE
A pink apron, a pan of spaghetti.
(See NATIONAL AFFAIRS)

Number 12

▼ **Source C** *Milt Hinton in* Memories of Al Capone.

"People in Chicago back then looked on Al Capone as a Robin Hood – he helped the poor. My uncle worked for him. He had a dry cleaning place and Capone used it as a headquarters for selling alcohol … Capone sold my uncle the alcohol for $12 a gallon and we'd sell it to people for $18 a gallon."

WISE UP WORD

● infamous

WORK

1 Look at **Source A**.
   a What was the 'popular demand' that Capone supplied?
   b Capone called himself a 'businessman'. Can you think of any other words to describe him?
   c What point is Capone making in this statement?

2 Look at **Source B**.
   a Are you surprised to see Al Capone on the front cover of a leading magazine? Give reasons for your answer.
   b What does it tell you about the way in which Capone was regarded by many Americans in the 1920s?

3 Imagine you are a reporter for *Time* magazine in 1930. You have been given the job of interviewing 'Big Al' for the March 1930 edition of this top-selling magazine. Capone has stated that he will only answer ten questions.
   i) Work out your ten questions (and remember not to offend him!).
   ii) Work with a partner (or on your own if you prefer) to write out the sort of answers you think Capone may have given.

FACT *Great shot Al!*

Al Capone was shot only once … he shot himself in the leg by mistake! When playing golf, he always kept a gun in his golf bag. Once, when picking up his bag, his gun went off accidentally.

The Monkey Trial

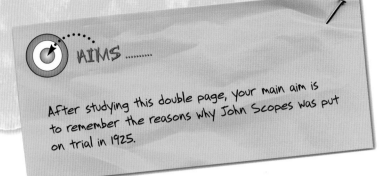

AIMS

After studying this double page, your main aim is to remember the reasons why John Scopes was put on trial in 1925.

In July 1925, a 24-year-old Biology teacher named John Scopes went on trial in Tennessee, one of America's southern states. His trial caused a media sensation, appearing all over America in magazines and newspapers – it was even broadcast live on the radio, a world first! His crime? He had been caught teaching Biology in a Biology lesson! This is the amazing story of the Scopes Trial, also known, even today, by millions of Americans as the 'Monkey Trial'.

The 1920s was an age of new ideas, new fashions, new inventions and new ways of living. This frightened many people. Some longed for a time when things were more stable, when ideas and theories about the world in which they lived didn't change so much.

One idea that had swept across America in the late 1800s and early 1900s was Charles Darwin's **theory of evolution**. He argued that life on earth began many millions of years ago and developed – or evolved – slowly into its present form. Human beings, he wrote, gradually evolved from apes over millions of years. For many people all over the world, not just in America, this was too much. Darwin was suggesting that there did not need to be a God to explain human existence!

The Bible Belt states

Many Americans are very religious people. In fact, several states in the south and mid-west – Tennessee, Arkansas, Alabama, Georgia and Kansas, for example – are known as the 'Bible Belt' states. People in these states go to church regularly and believe that everything in the Bible is true. When the Bible tells them that God created the world in five days and on the sixth day created human beings in his own image, they believe it. Darwin's theory opposes this view totally, claiming that life on earth, including humans, evolved slowly – man *wasn't* created in one day. By the 1920s, Darwin's theory was being taught as part of Biology lessons in most

of America's classrooms. By 1924, six states in the 'Bible Belt' felt that enough was enough. They decided to put a stop to this new theory that tried to undermine the Bible and passed laws making it illegal for teachers to teach the theory of evolution.

A few days later, John Scopes decided to put the law to the test in Tennessee, one of the states that had banned Darwin's theory. He taught it to a class of 14-year-olds and agreed to let his friend sue him for breaking the law.

The trial

The trial attracted the attention of the world's press, which billed it as a contest between America's old, traditional, religious values and more modern, ever-changing views on life. Both sides hired top lawyers – Scopes was represented by America's most famous lawyer, Clarence Darrow (an **atheist**) and the prosecution was led by William Jennings Bryan, a deeply religious man who had run for presidency three times.

▼ **Source A** *John Scopes (front row, light suit) surrounded by his legal team. His main lawyer, Clarence Darrow, is pictured on the left holding his famous white hat.*

There was little doubt that Scopes was guilty so the defence team instead focused on the arguments for and against evolution. As a result, it became known as the 'Monkey Trial'. Darrow continually tried to make fun of those who believed that the Bible was true, even calling Bryan as a witness and ridiculing his beliefs about Christianity (see **Source D**). Eventually, the judge had to step in and refused to allow the questions to continue. Bryan was taken ill and died five days later.

After a ferocious trial, the jury returned their verdict – Scopes was guilty and fined $100. However, Scopes and his supporters always claimed they had won a moral victory because they had demonstrated that some laws were worth breaking when they pose a threat to a person's freedom of speech and thought.

▼ **Source B** *Billy Sunday, a popular speaker, attacking the teaching of the theory of evolution in schools, 1925. Those who believed in the biblical explanation of the creation of the world were called* **fundamentalists**. *A fundamentalist is a person of any religion who believes the events described in their holy book, for example, the Bible or the Qur'an, are true and should not be questioned. Those who believed in Darwin's theory were known as* **evolutionists**.

" If anyone wants to teach that God-forsaken, hell-born, bastard theory of evolution, then let him … but do not expect the Christian people of this country to pay for the teaching of a rotten stinking professor who gets up there and teaches our children to forsake [abandon] God. "

▼ **Source C** *The Tennessee Anti-Evolution Law, 1925. Interestingly, after the Scopes Trial, the law was never used again and was removed soon after.*

" It is unlawful for any teacher to teach any theory that denies the story of the divine creation of man as taught in the Bible, and to teach instead that man had descended from a lower order of animals. "

▼ **Source D** *From the Monkey Trial, when Darrow cross-examined Bryan.*

Bryan: I believe everything in the Bible should be accepted.

Darrow: Do you believe in Jonah and the whale?

Bryan: You are talking miracles. It is easy to believe the miracle of Jonah.

Darrow: Do you believe Joshua made the sun stand still?

Bryan: I believe what the Bible says.

Darrow: Do you think the sun was made on the fourth day?

Bryan: Yes.

Darrow: Did Eve really come from Adam's rib?

Bryan: Yes.

Darrow: When did God create the world?

Bryan: In 4004BC.

Darrow: So you are saying there are no civilisations on this earth that go back beyond 5000 years?

Bryan: I am not satisfied by any evidence I have seen.

WISE UP WORDS

- theory of evolution   fundamentalists   evolutionists   atheist

WORK

1 **a** Why did John Scopes face trial in July 1925? In your answer, make sure you mention:
   - the theory of evolution • the 'Bible Belt'
   - the Tennessee Anti-Evolution Law.

   b Why do you think the trial became known as the 'Monkey trial'?

   c In what way did the trial show how some Americans were intolerant of other points of view?

2 Look at **Source D**. Explain why Darrow asked these questions. Do you think he got the answers he wanted?

3 Write a press report for the 'Monkey Trial'. In your report, include: • an interesting news headline • the arguments for the theory of evolution • the arguments against it • the reason for the trial … and the outcome.

Were Sacco and Vanzetti guilty?

AIMS

When studying these pages, try to:
- work out all the different reasons why Sacco and Vanzetti were brought to trial in 1921;
- form an opinion of your own as to whether they were guilty or not.

In April 1920, a robbery took place at a shoe factory in South Braintree, Massachusetts. The robbers stole $15 000 and shot two of the staff dead. A month later, two Italian-born immigrants – Nick Sacco and Bart Vanzetti – were arrested and charged with the robbery and murders. Their trial began in May 1921 and lasted 45 days. In July, the jury found them guilty and the judge sentenced them to 'death by electric chair'. But were Sacco and Vanzetti really guilty? Or were they just innocent victims who suffered because many Americans were becoming tired – and scared – of the millions of immigrants pouring into the country?

By the 1920s, the American government had started to reduce the number of immigrants they were letting into America. One reason for limiting immigration was fear. In Russia, a political group called the **Communists** had overthrown – and later killed – their rulers. The Communists now ran Russia and Americans feared that something like that could happen in America – especially as America had let in nearly 1.5 million Russians in the past few years. The fear of Communism grew further when Alexander Mitchell Palmer, the man in charge of America's law and police, was the target of a terrorist attack. A bomb ripped out the front of his house and next to the limbs of the suicide bomber was a newspaper called *Plain Words* – it was a Communist newspaper! Later that year, an unidentified bomber blew up 30 people in New York. No one was ever found guilty of this crime – but people's fear of Communism increased further.

As well as Communists, the **anarchists** were another group greatly feared in the 1920s. Anarchists believe that countries should not be ruled by organised governments with set laws and rules, but by a system where everyone rules themselves through voluntary cooperation. Americans felt they had good reason to fear anarchists – in 1901, an anarchist called Leon Franz Czolgosz shot dead US President William McKinley!

Nick Sacco and Bart Vanzetti were not only Italian immigrants who spoke very little English ... they were both anarchists too!

Study the evidence for and against them at their trial. Were they really guilty or just innocent scapegoats of a public who hated immigrants and anarchists?

▼ **Source A** *Sacco and Vanzetti in prison, 1921. There were demonstrations in major cities against the verdict – the American Embassy in Paris was even bombed.*

▼ **Source B**

EVIDENCE AGAINST SACCO AND VANZETTI

- 61 eyewitnesses identified them as the killers.
- Both men were carrying loaded guns when arrested. The bullets were the same size as those that killed the two men.
- Both men 'acted guilty' when arrested and told some lies to the police.
- Vanzetti had a previous conviction for armed robbery in December 1919.

▼ **Source C**

EVIDENCE FOR THE DEFENCE

- 107 people confirmed that Sacco and Vanzetti were somewhere else on the night of the robbery/murders.

- Witnesses nearly all disagreed over what the two men were wearing on the night in question.

- Several other men confessed to the murders.

- It is no crime in America to carry a loaded gun. Sacco and Vanzetti said they carried one because they were worried about being attacked because of their political beliefs.

- Sacco and Vanzetti spoke poor English. Their lawyers argued they got confused under police questioning and lied as they thought they were being victimised because they were foreigners and anarchists.

▼ **Source D** *The judge, Webster Thayer, said this just after the trial. He also called them 'dagos', 'wops' (two derogatory words used to describe Italians) and 'sons of bitches'.*

"Did you see what I did to those anarchist bastards?"

▼ **Source E** *A top American lawyer said this about the judge in charge of the trial. 'Reds' was a word used to describe Communists and anarchists. In fact, this period of political intolerance at the start of the 1920s is known as the Red Scare.*

"I have known Judge Thayer all my life … he is a narrow-minded man; he is a half-educated man; he is an unintelligent man; he is full of prejudice; he is carried away by fears of Reds which has captured about 90% of the American people."

▼ **Source F** *Based on Bart Vanzetti's last statement, made just before he was executed.*

"I am not guilty of these crimes. I have never commit a crime in my life. I have never steal, never kill, never spilt blood. I do not wish any misfortune, even to a dog or snake. I am suffering because of my beliefs. I am suffering because I am an Italian. If you executed me two times more and I was born again, I would still live my life the same."

Despite years of public demonstrations, protests, legal arguments and appeals, the two men were executed by electric chair on 23 August 1927. In 1977, 50 years after their execution, the Governor of Massachusetts granted Sacco and Vanzetti a formal pardon and accepted that an unfair trial had taken place.

WISE UP WORDS

- Communist   anarchist   Red Scare

WORK

1 Give reasons why many Americans were scared of Reds in the 1920s.

2 Look at **Sources B** and **C**.

   a What were Sacco and Vanzetti accused of?

   b What were the main differences between the evidence for the prosecution and the evidence for the defence? Design a chart to help you to present your findings.

3 Look at **Sources D** and **E**.

   a What impression do you get of Judge Thayer by reading these two sources?

   b Do you think he would have given Sacco and Vanzetti a fair trial? Explain your answer.

4 Look at **Source F**.

   a Why, according to Vanzetti, were he and Sacco found guilty?

   b Is this statement a useful piece of evidence that helps us to decide whether the two men were guilty or not? Explain your answer carefully.

5 Why do <u>you</u> think Sacco and Vanzetti were executed … and do you think they would have been executed today?

Have you been learning?

TASK 1: HUNT THE HERO!

Draw this puzzle in your book and fill in the answers to the clues. A name will reveal itself in the middle (clue 17). Write a sentence or two about this person.

17

1 ▸
2 ▸
3 ▸
4 ▸
5 ▸
6 ▸
7 ▸
8 ▸
9 ▸
10 ▸
11 ▸
12 ▸
13 ▸
14 ▸
15 ▸
16 ▸

Clues:

1 City where Al Capone made his name

2 Silent comedy film star

3 Young, independent woman

4 One of America's two main political parties

5 Rule book of the KKK

6 Nickname of John Scope's trial

7 Surname of one of the most famous jazz singers of all

8 A line on which cars were produced

9 Nickname for Henry Ford's T model

10 The Jazz _____ – first talking film

11 Henry Ford's son

12 One of America's two main political parties

13 Hit 60 home runs in the 1927 World Series

14 Alvin '____' Kelly

15 Alvin sat on these for long periods of time!

16 Ban on alcohol

TASK 2: WHAT'S IN A NAME?

Many 'labels' have been used to describe America in the 1920s: 'The Roaring Twenties', 'The Jazz Age', 'The Age of Wonderful Nonsense', 'The New Era', 'The Age of Excess' and 'The New Freedom' are just six of these labels.

a For each of the six labels, write a paragraph explaining why you think it is a suitable way to describe the 1920s (one has been started for you).

The age of excess – 'excess' means to have gone further than ever before and exceed the limits of what is seen as acceptable. In the 1920s, many people did this. More people owned cars than ever before. They bought consumer goods – radios, refrigerators, vacuum cleaners and so on – on credit and spent more than they had ever done. Women, especially the flappers, pushed the boundaries and behaved in ways they had never behaved before. They shocked some people by…

b When you have explained why you think each label has been used to describe America in the 1920s, write down which one you think is most suitable. Give reasons for your choice.

TASK 3: 'THE BAR-ROOM OR THE BOY'?

Study this postcard carefully. It was produced in 1918 by the Anti-Saloon League.

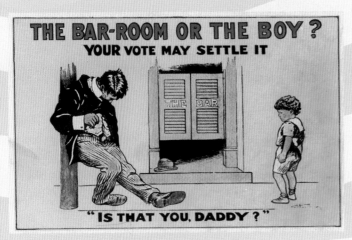

a What was the Anti-Saloon League?

b For what reasons, according to this poster, did the League want to ban alcohol?

c Write a sentence explaining each of these words, which are associated with the ban on alcohol in the 1920s. You may not use more than ten words in each explanation.

i) speakeasy

ii) moonshine

iii) bootleggers

iv) racketeering

d Why was Prohibition eventually repealed (ended)?

TASK 4: A MATTER OF OPINION

These people represent some of the different groups in America in the 1920s.

A flapper

A farmer with a small amount of land

A car worker at Ford's factory

A Black American living in a large city

A Russian immigrant

A middle-class housewife

a For each character, write a sentence or two describing their feelings about America in the 1920s – did the 1920s mean good or bad times for them?

b What other types of people could you include? What might they say?

TASK 5: QUESTION TIME

Look at these genuine GCSE questions carefully. Why not try to complete one, two or even all of them as a revision exercise? In brackets after each question, you will find the pages of this book where there is information that might refresh your memory.

- Describe developments in the motor car industry in the USA during the 1920s. (pages 16–19)

- What discrimination did Black Americans suffer during the 1920s? (pages 20–23)

- Explain why the lives of women changed in the 1920s. (pages 24–25)

- Describe the cinema industry in the USA during the 1920s. (pages 30–31)

- The following were reasons why American industry boomed in the 1920s:

  i) the effects of the First World War;

  ii) Republican policies;

  iii) new methods of production.

Which of these reasons do you think was the *most* important? Explain your answer, referring to i, ii and iii. (pages 12–15)

- Explain why American farmers faced problems during the 1920s. (pages 12–15)

- Explain why Prohibition was introduced. (pages 32–35)

- Why was Prohibition repealed? (pages 32–35)

- 'The most serious problem faced by American society in the 1920s was organised crime.' Do you agree with this statement? Explain your answer. (pages 32–39)

- What were the main features of the 'Roaring Twenties'?

- How much did American society change during the 1920s?

'Anyone ... ought to be rich'

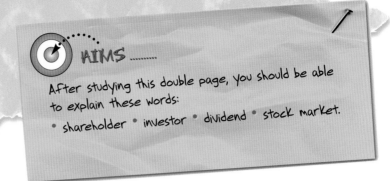

AIMS

After studying this double page, you should be able to explain these words:
• shareholder • investor • dividend • stock market.

In 1928, Herbert Hoover became President of America. He won the election easily. His political party, the Republicans, had been in power for over seven years and during that time, the boom times had swept across much of America. Hoover told Americans that they had more luxuries, better homes, nicer clothes and fuller bank accounts than any other country. He even said that 'Americans today are nearer to the final triumph over poverty than ever before. The poor man is vanishing from among us'.

So why did Hoover make such a prediction about the end of poverty? On what evidence was his speech based? And why, in just six months, was Hoover's speech seen as one of the worst predictions in American history?

Hoover's prediction was based on simple facts, brought to him by his advisors. On average, the wages of American workers had risen by 11% between 1921 and 1928. During the same period, the average working week dropped from 47.4 to 44.2 hours per week. So people, on average, worked less and earned more. Also, throughout the 1920s, ordinary Americans had all sorts of new inventions (the motor car, radio and so on), new forms of entertainment (jazz clubs, cinemas and so on) and new fashions to choose from. Hoover believed that with a lot of hard work and a bit of good fortune, anyone could make money – and he pointed to the **stock market** as one of his examples.

So how does the stock market work?

- To set up a company you need money – for wages, equipment, land and so on.

- Most companies get this from **investors**. In return, investors own a share of the company. They become **shareholders**.

- A shareholder makes money by:

  i) receiving a share of the company profits – a **dividend** – each year;

  ii) selling their share for a higher price than they paid. A shareholder will get more money than they paid for their share if the company

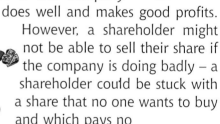

  does well and makes good profits. However, a shareholder might not be able to sell their share if the company is doing badly – a shareholder could be stuck with a share that no one wants to buy and which pays no dividends!

- Shares are bought and sold on the stock market ('stock' is another word for a share). In America, the country's stock market is in New York, on Wall Street.

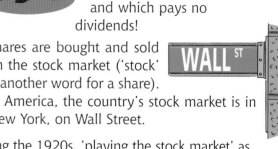

During the 1920s, 'playing the stock market' as it was known, became a national craze. Several million people, not just the rich, but ordinary Americans, bought shares in all sorts of companies ... and made money by selling them – only to buy more shares to try to make more money. Perhaps it seemed that Hoover's prediction of an end to poverty would soon come true (see **Sources A**, **B** and **C**).

▼ Source A *John J Raskob, Director of General Motors, 1928. Gambling on the stock market, often with borrowed money, was called* **speculation***.*

> "If a man buys $15 worth of shares a month, he will, at the end of 20 years, have at least $80 000 and an income from investments of $400 a month. I am firm in my belief that anyone can not only be rich, but ought to be rich."

▼ Source B *The price of shares in ten American companies. From which company would you have liked to have bought $100 worth of shares in 1928? How much would your shares be worth if you sold them in September 1929?*

COMPANY	3 March 1928 COST OF ONE SHARE (CENTS)	3 September 1929 COST OF ONE SHARE (CENTS)
American Can	77	182
Anaconda Copper	54	162
Electric Bond and Share	90	204
General Electric Company	129	396
General Motors	140	182
New York Central	160	256
Radio	94	505
US Steel	138	279
Westinghouse E & M	92	313
Woolworth	181	251

Millions of Americans agreed with Hoover when he said that the end of poverty was in sight: none more so than the millions who had made money from the stock market. In 1920, there had been only four million people who owned shares – by 1929, there were five times as many! For a while, it seemed that every investor – the housewife, the car worker, the shopkeeper, the chauffeur and the factory owner – won when playing the stock market!

WISE UP WORDS

- investor   shareholder   dividend
  stock market   speculation

▼ Source C *An investor makes money on the stock market.*

WORK

1. Test your understanding of this double page by writing a sentence or two about each of the following:
   • stock market • investor • shareholder • dividend

2. President Hoover believed that 'the poor man is vanishing'. What do you think made him think this?

3. Why did Americans invest money in shares in the 1920s? Give a full explanation, in your own words, of how someone might make a profit from 'playing the stock market'.

4. Look at **Source B**.
   a. How much would 100 shares in 'Radio' have cost in March 1928? (Clue: multiply the share price of 94 cents by 100.)
   b. How much would 100 shares in 'Radio' be worth if you sold them in September 1929? (Clue: multiply the share price of 505 cents by 100 – remember there are 100 cents to a dollar.)
   c. How much profit would you have made?

GCSE Question time

- Why did Americans invest money in the stock market in the 1920s?

Why did Wall Street 'crash'?

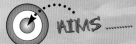

AIMS ....

Over the next four pages, aim to understand:

- Why so many people tried to sell their shares in October 1929;
- how 'Black Thursday' got its name;
- how banks work ... and why many had failed by 1930.

During the 1920s, it seemed as if the stock market was an easy way to get rich. Anyone could buy shares, watch their value rise and then sell the shares later at a higher price (see **Source A**). Banks were more than willing to lend money to these share speculators (another word for an investor) knowing that they would get their money back soon – with interest!

▼ **Source A** Big profits could be made by 'playing the stock market'.

"If an investor bought 1000 shares in Radio [a company that made radios … obviously!] in March 1928, they would have cost $940. The shares were 94 cents each. If they sold the shares in September 1929, then they would have been able to get $5050 for them because the share price had risen to $5.05 for each one. That's a profit of $4110."

However, disaster was just around the corner. Not all Americans had the wealth to buy the goods made by companies and there was a limit to the number of cars, radios, telephones and refrigerators the more wealthy people could buy. After all, a family home is highly unlikely to have more than one oven, vacuum cleaner or refrigerator. American factories were **overproducing** – making goods faster than they could sell them – and profits were beginning to fall!

To begin with, in September 1929, one or two cautious people began to sell their shares. They were worried that they wouldn't get their share of company profits at the end of the year. As word spread about the falling profits of leading American companies, more and more people began to sell their shares. The result was astonishing. Shareholders realized that their shares (which were only pieces of paper entitling them to a share of company profits) were only worth something if someone was willing to buy them. As they tried to turn their shares into cash, they dropped their share price to attract a buyer. On 24 October 1929, 13 million shares were sold on the Wall Street Stock Exchange (five times as many as on a normal day) and share prices in nearly all companies began to drop. The price of a share in the General Electric Company fell from $3.15 to $2.83 and shares in Radio fell by 24 cents. Some investors called this **Black Thursday**; others called it the 'Crash'.

Once the rush to sell began, the situation got worse and worse. People just didn't want their shares – they wanted their cash instead – so they dropped their prices more and more to attract a buyer. On Tuesday 29 October, there was another mad panic to sell shares – at any price. Sixteen million shares were sold during the day and the average price of shares dropped 40 cents. Shareholders lost a total of $8000 million (see **Source B**)!

▼ **_Source B_** *The cost of one share in ten American companies. Imagine if you had borrowed money from a bank to buy 100 Radio shares in September 1929 … and then tried to sell them in November when the bank asked for its money back!*

COMPANY	3 September 1929 COST OF ONE SHARE (CENTS)	13 November 1929 COST OF ONE SHARE (CENTS)
American Can	182	86
Anaconda Copper	162	70
Electric Bond and Share	204	50
General Electric Company	396	168
General Motors	182	36
New York Central	256	160
Radio	505	28
US Steel	279	150
Westinghouse E & M	313	102
Woolworth	251	57

FACT *Suicide!*

The shares of Union Cigar fell from $113 per share to $4 per share. The president of the company committed suicide by jumping from a top-floor window of a New York hotel.

As the year went on, things got even worse. Many Americans had borrowed money from banks to buy shares, hoping to pay back their loans when the shares rose in price. But when share prices fell, investors couldn't sell their shares for a high enough price to be able to pay their bank back in full. If enough customers couldn't pay back their loans, the banks went bankrupt. When this happened, ordinary people who had savings in the bank lost all their money (see **Source C**). In 1929 alone, 659 banks went bust!

▼ **_Source C_** *Author Geoffrey Pensett talking on the TV series* America's Century.

"There was a janitor called George Gallies who had $1000 in the Bank of the United States. It had taken Gallies 40 years to save $1000. After spending two nights and two days in the pouring rain outside this shuttered, locked bank, beating on the walls with his hands in frustration, he realized he was never going to see ten cents of his money. So he went back to the basement where he lived and he hanged himself in despair. That's what bank failures did — they crushed hundreds of thousands of ordinary people like George Gallies."

▲ **_Source D_** *A photograph of worried investors on Wall Street taken on Black Thursday, 1929.*

▼ **Source E** *New York, October 1929. A ruined shareholder tries to raise money quickly.*

FACT *How does a bank work?*

American banks in the 1920s, which were often small, one-town operations, worked like this – there were two parts to the bank:

*Savings – people put their savings into the bank; the bank rewarded them each year with an interest payment, for example, 5% of what you saved. If you saved $1000, the bank would give you a $50 interest bonus.

*Loans – people could borrow money from the bank, but would have to pay the bank an interest payment each year, for example, 10% of the loan. If you borrowed $1000, you would have to pay back $1100.

In 1929, the problems started when people couldn't pay back their loans because they'd swapped their money for new worthless shares. The bank had loaned out all the 'savings' money to those who wanted loans. The money had gone ... and banks went bankrupt.

▼ **Source G** *Luigi Barzini, an Italian immigrant, remembers the Wall Street Crash. He was a schoolboy at the time.*

"Famous firms went bankrupt. Stockbrokers jumped to their deaths from the tops of skyscrapers. The price of shares sank even lower … people I knew were down and out. Some put their houses up for sale (a useless act as no one was buying anything) or boarded them up and left because they could no longer afford to live there. Shops sold their stock at clearance sales and closed forever. An old couple who lived not far from us lost everything in the Crash. It was too late for them to start life again so they committed suicide."

▲ **Source F** *Wall Street after the Crash. Worried crowds have gathered outside the Stock Exchange on 29 October 1929, trying to find out what has happened to the value of their shares. At one point, the police arrived to keep order.*

WORK

1 a Why did some people begin to sell their shares in September 1929?

  b What happens to share prices as more and more people sell their shares?

  c What happened on 'Black Thursday'?

  d Why did many banks go 'bankrupt' as a result of the Crash?

2 Look at **Source B**.

  a Imagine you had bought 100 shares in 'Radio' in September 1929. How much would you have paid for them?

  b How much would you be able to get if you sold your 100 shares after the Crash, in November 1929?

  c How much money would you have lost on these shares?

3 Look at **Source E**.

  a What evidence is there in this photograph that the seller of this car made lots of money on the stock market before the Crash?

  b Why do you think the man was trying to sell his car so urgently?

  c Do you think he found a buyer? Give reasons for your answer.

4 What do **Sources C**, **D**, **E**, **F** and **G** tell us about the effects of the Crash on some people?

GCSE Question time

• What was the Wall Street Crash?

WISE UP WORDS

• overproduction   Black Thursday

How did the Wall Street Crash lead to the Great Depression?

AIMS

After studying these two pages, you should be able to:
- explain how the Wall Street Crash affected different sections of American society;
- explain how the Wall Street Crash led to the Great Depression.

The shock waves of the Wall Street Crash were soon felt throughout America. Some American businesses were already in trouble before the Crash – they were producing too many products that they couldn't sell (there is a limit to the amount of cars, radios and fridges people can afford to buy!) – but after 1929, things got much worse. In fact, by 1930, most Americans were starting to use the word 'depression' to describe America's problems. A depression is a time in a country's history when things are bad – factories close, banks fail and unemployment reaches record levels – and there seems no end to the problems. America's depression was so bad that people even started calling it the **Great Depression** – they said that they had never known it so bad – the country had gone from 'boom' to 'bust' in just a few short years.

Read the following stories carefully. They show the effects of the Wall Street Crash on some Americans.

'I lost a fortune during the Crash. I tried to pay my bank loan back by selling my car but it wasn't enough. I can't even pay next month's rent on my apartment. I think I'll have to move onto the streets!'

'We loaned out so much money in the 1920s. Many spent it buying shares. Now they can't pay us back and we are close to going bankrupt. I'll probably lose my job. Other banks have already closed. I feel sorry for people who've saved with us for years - we loaned their money out and now they'll never get it back.'

BANK OF NEW YORK

BANK MANAGER

> **FACT** *Bankrupt*
>
> One of America's biggest banks – the Bank of the United States in New York – went bankrupt in December 1930. 400 000 people saved with the bank – almost one-third of New Yorkers. They lost all their savings.

'My factory makes radios, thousands of them every month. We've made so many that we can't sell them. After the Crash, people could afford even less. I can't sell them abroad either because foreign countries tax American goods heavily - we do it to their goods too! I'm going to have to cut production, then wages and eventually I'm going to have to sack workers.'

'I've just lost my job in the car factory. Americans bought 4.5 million cars in 1927 - but we're not even going to sell a quarter of that total this year. People have no money - they either lost it in the Crash, have recently lost their own job, or couldn't afford a car in the first place. I just heard that our local hairdresser has closed down - people are even getting their hair cut at home.'

WISE UP WORDS

- underconsumption   Great Depression

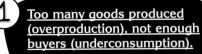

I've been losing money for years. New farming methods meant we produced too much food - so we dropped prices to sell some of it. The bank is desperate to get me to pay my equipment loans back too. With less money coming in, I can't really afford to pay my debts or my mortgage. I'm close to losing my farm - and sacking all my poor farm workers.'

'I lost a bit in the Crash - not too much though. A few of my factories are struggling but I have lots of property and land to keep me going. I've had to make some changes though - I've sacked my chauffeur and cleaners. I drive myself now and my wife does the cleaning.'

▼ **_Source A_** *The economic effect of overproduction, **underconsumption** and the Wall Street Crash.*

① **Too many goods produced (overproduction), not enough buyers (underconsumption).**
- people who could afford goods already had them
- poorer people – some farmers, black workers and so on – couldn't afford new goods anyway

② **Some companies cut back on costs**
- some workers were sacked
- some wages were cut
- fewer goods produced in some factories
- profits dropped

③a Now there were fewer workers with less money

③b Lower profits led some shareholders to panic and sell shares fast
Wall Street Crash
- millions lose money

④ Fewer goods were bought as people had less money

⑤ Companies closed down because people were buying less
- more workers sacked
- people had less money to spend

DEPRESSION   DEPRESSION

WORK

1 **a** How were the following affected by the Wall Street Crash? i) ordinary shareholders ii) banks iii) factory owners iv) factory workers v) farmers vi) the very rich

  b Who was worst affected? Who was least affected? Give reasons for your opinions.

2 Create a flow chart to show how the Wall Street Crash pushed America towards the Great Depression. You can try to organise your chart yourself and explain it in your own words or use some (or all) of the sentences below ... but you'll have to arrange them in the right order.

The first one has been done for you:

i | Many lost money in the Crash. Also, as banks asked for loan money back, people spent even less on consumer goods.

The rest are mixed up:

ii | As unemployment rose, there was even less money to buy goods.

iii | As less money was spent, company profits fell.

iv | Even more companies went bust; more workers became unemployed, creating a further fall in demand for goods.

v | As company profits fell, they were forced to pay lower wages or sack workers.

GCSE Question time
- Explain the effects of the Wall Street Crash on the American economy.

'Buddy, can you spare a dime?': the Great Depression in words and pictures

Many Americans were devastated by the Great Depression. Millions of workers lost their jobs as factories closed and businesses shut. More job losses meant people stopped spending – so then more factories and businesses closed down. In the steel-making city of Cleveland, 50% of workers were unemployed by 1931. In Toledo, a car-making town, it was 80%. At night, the parks were full of the homeless and unemployed – in the day they queued for bread and soup dished out by charity workers. Study the following sources carefully. They're an incredible insight into how the Great Depression affected the American people.

▼ **Source A** *Unemployed workers sit outside a closed-down café in New York, 1930. Note the young girl on the right sitting next to her dad. Some of these men were architects, but during the Depression, building construction and design fell by 92%.*

▼ **Source B** *Unemployment in the USA, 1929–1933. In New York alone, 10 000 of New York's 25 000 manufacturing firms (companies that made things) had closed down by 1932. The percentage figure represents the unemployed as a percentage of the labour force (those able to work). In other words, in 1933, nearly 25%, or one out of four people, were unable to find work. Some historians say it was higher, more like one out of two.*

Unemployed in millions

Year	Unemployed	Percentage
1929	1.6m	3.2%
1930	4.3m	8.7%
1931	8.0m	15.9%
1932	12.0m	23.6%
1933	14.0m	24.9%

▾ **Source C** *A queue of homeless and hungry people waits for free charity food in New York on Christmas Day, 1931. These queues were called* **breadlines**. *In 1932, the charity organisation YMCA was giving away 12 000 free meals a day in one small district of New York.*

▾ **Source D** *Marty Glickman, a famous sports writer, remembering his childhood.*

"On one occasion, my father came home and asked what was for dinner and my mother said, 'There's nothing'. How could that be? How could there be nothing? It was one of the few times in my life that I was scared."

▾ **Source E** *250 000 Americans stopped paying their mortgages in 1932. Within weeks, most were evicted from their homes and many took to living on the streets. Some travelled the country looking for work, whilst others moved to waste ground and built shacks with cardboard boxes, scrap metal, old cloth and pallets. These camps – with no proper toilets or washing facilities – were called* **Hoovervilles**, *a sarcastic reference to the President, Herbert Hoover, whom many felt wasn't doing enough to help people. The children in this photograph, whose parents probably had decent jobs until recently, are shown with signs that poke fun at the President.*

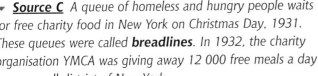

▼ **Source F** *Written by a modern historian, 1997.*

"Hoover didn't think the Depression would last long. 'Prosperity [wealth] is just around the corner', he told a group of businessmen in 1932. In speeches, he repeated his belief that there was nothing basically wrong … many people who had voted for Hoover in 1928 now said, 'In Hoover we trusted, now we are busted.' They used his name in ways that showed they blamed him for the Depression. 'Hoovervilles' was the name they gave to shanty towns made of rubbish, where homeless, out-of-town people lived. 'Hoover Stew' was the soup given out by the charity workers."

▼ **Source G** *From The Grapes of Wrath, a novel written by John Steinbeck in 1939. It tells the story of a poor farming family from Oklahoma who travel to California during the Great Depression in search of a new life.*

"There was a Hooverville on the edge of every town … the houses were tents, weed-thatched enclosures, paper houses, a great junk pile. The man drove his family in and became a citizen of Hooverville — always they were called Hooverville … if he had no tent, he went to the city dump and brought back cartons and built a house made of corrugated paper. When the rains came, the house melted and washed away."

▼ **Source H** *From New Republic magazine, February 1933.*

"Last summer in the hot weather, when the smell was sickening and the flies were thick, there were a hundred people a day coming to the dumps … a widow who used to do housework and laundry, but now had no work at all, fed herself and her 14-year-old son on garbage. Before she picked up the meat, she would always take off her glasses so that she couldn't see the maggots."

▼ **Source I** *With so many people unemployed, farmers couldn't get good prices for their food. As a result, many farmers couldn't afford to pay their mortgages and by 1932, one in twenty farmers had been evicted from their farms. To make matters worse for the farmers who managed to keep hold of their land, a drought combined with bad farming methods turned the land into what was called the* **Dust Bowl**. *Huge dust storms simply blew away millions of areas of dry topsoil, making it impossible to farm the land properly. Hundreds of small landowners, like the family in this photograph, loaded all their belongings onto their car or truck and moved away.*

"They streamed over the mountains, hungry and restless as ants, scurrying to find work to do – to lift, to push, to pull, to pick, to cut – anything for food. 'The kids are hungry. We've got no place to live.' Like ants scurrying for work and most of all for land…. They were hungry and they were fierce. And they hoped to find a home and they found only hatred."

▲ **Source J** *From The Grapes of Wrath by John Steinbeck. Thousands of farms were destroyed by high winds and drought, especially in the states of Oklahoma and Arkansas. In total, 350 000 'Okies' and 'Arkies' made their way towards the rich farming states of California and Oregon, hoping to work on fruit farms. However, most were disappointed – some towns banned the migrants, putting up signs saying 'Okies go home' – and the fruit farmers themselves were suffering too – people simply couldn't afford as much fruit!*

▼ **Source K** *Part of a very popular song from the 1930s called 'Buddy, can you spare a dime?' A dime is a type of American coin.*

"They used to tell me I was
    building a dream,
And so I followed the mob,
When there was earth to plough or
    guns to bear
I was always there – right on the
    job.

They used to tell me I was building
    a dream,
With peace and glory ahead.
Why should I be standing in line
Just waiting for bread?

Say – don't you remember, they
    called me Al,
It was Al all the time.
Say – don't you remember, I'm your
    pal,
Buddy, can you spare a dime?"

▼ **Source L** A photograph of a Black American family outside their home. In both towns and cities, Black Americans suffered badly – they were often the first to be sacked and the last to be hired if a number of new job vacancies appeared. In some businesses, the black workers were replaced with white workers!

WISE UP WORDS

● breadline   Dust Bowl   Hooverville

▼ **Source M** *A letter written to the President by a white woman during the Depression. The poverty of many white people increased their racist opinions and led them to turn against Black Americans even more.*

dear sur,

...it looks like you could do something to help out the poor white people the negroes can get work where the poor white man cannot ... there is a negroe working in the post office and white men can't get a job to feed his family ... and negroes being worked ever where instead of white men it don't look that it is rite and is not rite...'

▼ **Source N** *Written by a modern historian, showing how America's Great Depression turned into a world depression.*

"America's Great Depression affected the world. During the 1920s, the American government lent money to other countries and American citizens bought their goods. When the Depression hit, America stopped giving cash to other countries and asked for their old loans back. Also, now most American citizens couldn't afford their expensive German and British cars, Italian shoes or Japanese silk shirts. Businesses closed down in these countries too. Millions became unemployed. Hunger and poverty changed the way people thought and behaved. In some countries, like Germany, people began voting for political parties whose leaders promised them work if they were elected to power. One such party was called the Nazis."

So what did President Hoover do? Hoover remained convinced that America would recover soon. In January 1930, he said, 'We have now passed the worst'.

He eventually set up the Reconstruction Finance Corporation, which lent money to businesses in trouble and made some small loans to farmers. He also set up a huge road and dam building programme which created jobs in the construction industry. However, his policies came too late. In November 1932, there was a presidential election and Hoover hoped for re-election. He stood no chance – his time as President was about to end!

WORK

1 Look at **Source A**. Why do you think so many house builders, architects and designers were unemployed in the 1930s?

2 Look at **Source B**.
   a Copy out the chart neatly.
   b How many people were unemployed in 1929?
   c What proportion of the workforce was this?
   d How had this changed by 1933?

3 Look at **Source C**.
   a What does this source tell you about the number of people unemployed in New York?
   b Women, as well as men, were unemployed when this photograph was taken. So why do you think that only the men are queuing up in this breadline?

4 Look at **Sources E** and **F**.
   a What was a Hooverville?
   b Why did President Hoover do so little at first to help the unemployed?
   c How do you think Hoover felt about the names 'Hooverville' and 'Hoover stew'? Were these labels fair to him?

5 Look at **Sources I** and **J**.
   a What was the Dust Bowl?
   b Why were so many people, like the family photographed in **Source I**, leaving the countryside?
   c What were 'Okies' and why do you think they were treated so badly when they moved to other places?

6 Look at **Sources L** and **M**. What evidence is there in these two sources that Black Americans suffered worst of all during the Great Depression?

GCSE Question time
● What was the Great Depression?

President Hoover versus the Bonus Army: how close was a revolution?

AIMS

Aim to understand:
- What the Bonus Army wanted;
- how close America came to revolution in 1932.

After two years of Depression, many ordinary Americans didn't think their President, Herbert Hoover, was doing enough to help them. Some people joined together to organise protests, hoping to improve their conditions. Poor farmers in the state of Iowa used shotguns and pitchforks to chase away government officials who tried to evict farm owners who couldn't pay their mortgages. In Arkansas, 500 heavily armed starving farmers marched into the shopping centre of their local town and threatened to smash up shops unless they were given free food.

But the biggest protest by far took place in Washington, during the boiling hot summer of 1932. The situation in the country's capital city got so bad that the President barricaded himself inside a cupboard in his home, the White House.

So what caused the President to take such extreme action? How did he eventually deal with the protesters? And how close was America to revolution in the summer of 1932?

The men who caused such concern for President Hoover were ex-soldiers from the First World War. There were 25 000 of them in total and they were very hungry … and very angry! They had gone to Washington to ask the government to help them to survive the Depression by paying their war pensions – a $500 bonus – early. They had built a Hooverville just in front of the White House.

Hoover and the government refused to pay so the Bonus Army – as the ex-soldiers now called themselves – decided to stay. Hoover publicly called them 'criminals', which annoyed the ex-soldiers even more – despite the fact that Hoover himself knew that 95% were indeed veteran soldiers!

After a few tense days, Hoover called in the troops. Led by an army general called Douglas MacArthur, four companies of infantry, four mounted cavalry troops, a machine gun squad and six tanks attacked the protesters.

Two protesters and a baby (some ex-soldiers brought their families) were killed in the battle that followed. Pictures, like **Source F**, appeared in newspapers all over the country.

To many Americans, Hoover had had his last chance – there was a presidential election soon. To others, as the smoke from the burning Hooverville drifted over the nation's capital, it seemed as if America was near to a revolution.

▼ **Source A** *The President of the Wisconsin Farmers' Union, speaking in 1932.*

"Farmers are just ready to do anything … I honestly believe that if some of them could buy airplanes, they would come down here to Washington to blow you fellows up."

▼ **Source B** *A newspaper report from Indiana, 1931.*

"Around 1500 jobless men stormed the factory of the Fruit Growers Express Company here, demanding that they be given jobs to keep them from starving. The company's answer was to call the city police who used clubs to force the jobless to leave."

▼ **Source C** *From* A New Deal, America 1932–45.

"In Iowa … the Farmers' Union organised strikes to stop food from reaching the markets. Their aim was to create food shortages in the nearby towns, hoping that this would make food prices rise. If food prices rose, the farmers' income would rise too. So they blocked roads with chairs and logs and they smashed the windscreens of any trucks they caught being driven to market."

▼ **Source D** *General Douglas MacArthur, quoted in* The Memoirs of Herbert Hoover, *written by Hoover in 1953.*

"That mob was a bad-looking mob … beyond a shadow of a doubt, they were about to take over in some way. Had he [President Hoover] let it go on another week, I believe … our Government would have been very severely threatened."

▼ **Source E** *An eyewitness' account of the attack on the Bonus Army.*

"They came with their gas bombs and their bayonets. The troops fired the shacks on the edge of the camp. Tanks and soldiers guarded the bridge back into the city so that no protesters could get into Washington. They might disturb the sleep of a few of the Government's officials!"

▼ **Source F** *Police attacking members of the Bonus Army, Washington, 1932. Look for: i) the man (in a headlock) holding the American flag – why do you think he carried the flag? ii) The men in the Bonus Army (on the left) who have picked up bricks and pipes. iii) The policeman (on the right) who is picking up a baseball bat.*

WORK

1 Look at **Sources A**, **B** and **C**. Why do you think farmers were turning to such violent protest and making such severe threats?

2 **a** The *New York Evening Post* described the summer of 1932 as 'the most threatening time the Depression has brought upon America'. What, in particular, do you think made him write this?

  b Write down five facts about the Bonus Army and their time in Washington in the summer of 1932.

3 Look at **Source D**.

  a MacArthur led the government troops that attacked the Bonus Army protesters. Two protesters and a baby were killed. How does MacArthur justify his actions that day?

  b Is MacArthur a reliable witness when he says that the Bonus Army 'were about to take over in some way'? Give reasons for your answer.

4 What impact do you think the attack on the Bonus Army had on Hoover's election chances?

Have <u>you</u> been learning?

TASK 1: ANAGRAMS

In the word box below, you will find:

- A person who has bought shares
- The name of a share in a company's profits
- Another word for a share
- The street in which the New York stock exchange sits
- The month in which the Wall Street Crash took place
- Nickname for the day of the 'Crash'
- The US President at the time of the Wall Street Crash
- The official word for producing too many goods that people can't afford to buy
- The name given to the long period of high unemployment that followed the 'Crash'
- A queue of people wanting food
- A town made from rubbish
- A group of ex-soldiers who marched to Washington

All the answers are given below, but the words and letters have been mixed up. Can you unravel them?

> hhdrsoleear   ediinddv   tocks   lalw rtetse
> bcrtooe   klcba ashdtryu   rbrhtee vorohe
> nuoporverctiod   rndealbie   onsbu ryma
> voioerhvlel   eratg erpdsieosn

TASK 2: WHAT'S IN A NAME?

This photograph was taken in 1933 and shows a Hooverville near the dock in New York City. Can you see the man cooking on a barbecue?

a What was a Hooverville? In your answer, explain how Hoovervilles got their name.

b Why did the number of Hoovervilles grow and grow in the early years of the 1930s?

c Match each of the Hoover names to an explanation, then write them out in your book.

Hooverville	The cardboard with which people patched up the soles of their shoes.
Hoover stew	Old newspapers used for warmth.
Hoover blankets	Fruit sold by the unemployed on the streets.
Hoover apples	Shanty towns built on the outskirts of towns where the homeless sheltered.
Hoover leather	The thin soup distributed at charity kitchens.

TASK 3: DESPERATE TIMES

In 1932, a journalist travelled around America and wrote this about the things he saw:

> 'In the state of Washington, I was told that the forest fires raging in the region all summer were started by unemployed wood workers and bankrupt farmers in an attempt to earn a few honest dollars as fire fighters. The last thing I saw on the night I left Seattle was numbers of women searching for scraps of food in the rubbish piles ... while Oregon sheep farmers fed mutton [dead sheep meat] to buzzards [meat-eating birds], I saw men picking for meat scraps in the garbage cans in the cities of New York and Chicago ... we have overproduction and underconsumption at the same time in the same country.'

a According to the journalist, why were there so many fires in the state of Washington?

b Why do you think the sheep farmers fed the meat to buzzards rather than eat it?

c Why do you think the journalist mentioned men in New York and Chicago picking for meat scraps in the same sentence as the sheep farmers?

d What do you think the phrase 'overproduction and underconsumption at the same time in the same country' means?

TASK 4: ODD TWO OUT

Here are eight sentences. Each sentence has two errors. One is a spelling mistake; the other is a factual error. When you have spotted the mistakes, write the sentence out correctly.

a On Thursday 24 October 1928, shair prices on Wall Street fell faster and lower than at any other time before or since. Some called it Black Thursday; others called it the 'Crash'.

b Many people had borrowed money from banks to buy shares. When they couldn't pay back their loans, the bank closed down. In 1929 alone, six banks went bankrupped.

c As people spent less money, factories and buisnesses began to shut down. Unemployment had risen to 120 million by 1932.

d 250 000 Americans stopped paying their morgages and lost their homes in 1932. Some ended up living in shanty towns made from rubbish called 'Astonvillas'.

e The American President between 1926 and 1932 was called Herbert Hovver. Many resented him for not doing enough to help America to recover from the worst effects of the Great Depression.

f Problems in the early 1930s were made worse by the fact that huge areas of farmland were blown away by high winds. Thousands of farms were distroyed in an area known as 'the Dust Basin'.

g In the summer of 1932, thousands of ex-World War Two soldiers marched to Washington to protest about their penshuns. They were known as the Bonus Army.

h In December 1932, there was a Residential election. Herbert Hoover hoped to be re-elected. However, millions of Americans had turned against him by now.

TASK 5: QUESTION TIME

Look at these genuine GCSE questions carefully. Why not try to complete one, two or even all of them as a revision exercise? In brackets after each question, you will find the pages of this book where there is information that might refresh your memory.

- Why did Americans invest money in the stock market in the 1920s? (pages 46–47)

- What was the Wall Street Crash? (pages 48–51)

- Explain the effects of the Wall Street Crash on the American economy. (pages 52–59)

- What problems did the USA face in 1933? (pages 52–61)

- What was the Great Depression? (pages 52–61)

The 1932 election: who would you vote for?

AIMS

These four pages will help you to identify reasons:
- Why FDR won the 1932 election;
- Why HH lost the 1932 election.

Every four years, in November, an election is held for the post of President of the USA. The two main candidates for the 1932 election were Herbert Hoover (hoping to be re-elected) and Franklin Delano Roosevelt, also known as FDR. The election was taking place in the depths of the Depression – so what were their ideas for dealing with it? What was each candidate really like? What sort of lives had they led? And, of course, who won?

FACTFILE ON HOOVER

AGE: 58 years old (born in 1874 in Iowa)

BACKGROUND: Lost both parents by the age of eight. Brought up by two uncles. Became an office boy when he left school. Went to university at the age of 18 to study mine engineering. At 21, he began to work as a gold miner, working ten hours a day, seven days a week. Got several promotions and saved enough money to leave America and go to work in the gold mines of Australia. Travelled the world as a mining engineer, working hard to become a multi-millionaire by the age of 40. Retired from mining to go into politics.

POLITICAL PARTY: Hoover belonged to the Republican Party, traditionally favoured by businessmen and wealthier people. Republicans believed it wasn't the government's role to interfere too much in the everyday lives of its citizens (a policy called 'laissez faire' meaning leave alone). You may wish to go back to page 11 to refresh your memory on the Republican Party.

POLITICAL CAREER: Excellent early career in politics, doing a great job helping to feed starving people in Europe after the First World War. He became President in 1928 at a time when many Americans were making lots of money and could afford luxuries like cars, radios and telephones. He said that soon all Americans would have 'two cars in every garage and a chicken in every pot'.

IDEAS FOR DEALING WITH THE DEPRESSION: Didn't do much to begin with. Hoover thought of Americans as **rugged individuals**, people who could overcome any problem without help and achieve success through their own hard work (like he had!). As a result, he decided to leave America to recover on its own. Only after a few years of depression did he lend money to businesses and farms in trouble and make cash available to states to help their unemployed.

SPECIAL NOTES: Hoover was not a great public speaker and his belief in rugged individualism made him look uncaring. When he went out campaigning for votes, his 'election train' was often pelted with eggs and tomatoes. In one city, he was greeted with signs reading 'Hang Hoover'. During the election campaign, one newspaper reporter wrote, 'I don't know about rugged individuals, our tattered clothes make us look like ragged individuals'.

FACTFILE ON FDR

AGE: 50 (born in 1882 near New York).

BACKGROUND: An only child with very rich parents. Lived in a mansion. Spoilt by his mother and educated at home by private tutors until he was 14. Went to an expensive private school and then became a law student at Harvard, America's top university. He married his cousin, Eleanor, in 1905. He wasn't a particularly good lawyer so he decided to go into politics in 1910, aged 28.

POLITICAL PARTY: FDR belonged to the Democratic Party. This was a family tradition – his distant cousin, Teddy Roosevelt, had been America's Democrat President from 1901 to 1909. Turn to page 11 to refresh your memory on the Democratic Party.

POLITICAL CAREER: He had an important job organising the navy during the First World War. Nearly killed by polio, a spinal disease, in 1921. He spent the next five years fighting to recover but never fully regained the use of his legs. He used a wheelchair for the rest of his life. Went back into politics in 1928, becoming Governor of New York, a very important job.

IDEAS FOR DEALING WITH THE DEPRESSION:
As Governor of New York, he spent $20 million in tax money helping the unemployed – the first Governor of any state to do this. This, he told people, was how he intended to deal with the Depression if he became President. He promised America the three Rs:

- **R**elief – help for the old, sick, unemployed and homeless;
- **R**ecovery – government schemes to provide jobs;
- **R**eform – make America a better place for ordinary people and ensure a depression like this could not happen again.

He called his new ideas 'a **New Deal** for the American people' and without giving away too much detail, convinced people that it would lead to a better life. He took his message around the country, sometimes making 15 speeches a day, and his official campaign tune – the famous song 'Happy Days Are Here Again' – could be heard everywhere he went. The phrase 'New Deal' caught the imagination of the public and would lead him to one of the biggest election victories in American history. In FDR, people saw hope for the future – a man with a plan. His words made them feel that at last, someone was on their side!

SPECIAL NOTES: Many historians believe that FDR's illness and disability gave him empathy for the problems of ordinary people. He once wrote that his recovery from polio meant him spending 'two years in bed trying to move my big toe'. Voters liked FDR because he had managed to battle back from great personal difficulties – they thought he was a man with the right experience to help America recover from the Depression.

▼ **Source A** *This is a copy of a famous poster. Published by the Democratic Party, it makes fun of Republican candidate Herbert Hoover's 'do nothing' reputation. In many people's eyes, Hoover didn't act quickly enough to help people during the Depression – instead, he decided to 'leave alone' and tell people to 'keep smiling' because things would get better soon!*

Smile away the Depression

Smile us into Prosperity
wear a

SMILETTE!

This wonderful little gadget will
solve the problems of the Nation!

**APPLY NOW AT YOUR CHAMBER OF COMMERCE
OR YOUR REPUBLICAN NATIONAL COMMITTEE**

WARNING – Do not risk Federal arrest by looking glum!

▼ **Source B** *Herbert Hoover, October 1932.*

"This is more than a contest between two men. It is more than a contest between two political parties. It is a contest between two styles of government."

▼ **Source C** *Part of FDR's famous New Deal speech, July 1932.*

"I pledge [promise] you, I pledge myself, to a New Deal for the American people. This is more than a political campaign; it is a call to arms. Give me your help, not to win votes alone, but to win in this crusade to restore America."

▼ **Source D** *Election poster issued by supporters of FDR, 1932. FDR promised to end Prohibition, which made him very popular. It was certainly a vote winner. John Garner, the man on the right of the poster, was running as FDR's vice-President. He once described the job he would get as 'not worth a jug of warm spit'!*

FACT *'And the winner is...'*

FDR won a staggering victory. In 1932, there were 48 states in America – and 42 of them chose FDR. This was the biggest ever victory recorded in an American election!

▼ **Source E** *The historian, C Phillips, writing in* From the Crash to the Blitz.

"Roosevelt showed himself to the voters in every part of the country. He showed that his physical problems were no barrier to him. The result was all he could have hoped for. The country gained a picture of him as a smiling, warm-hearted man with the poise [calmness] and self-assurance [confidence] of an experienced politician. The thousands who saw him found his optimism infectious and exhilarating. As the earnest [serious], plodding defender of the existing government, Hoover was no match for Roosevelt's fast-paced attack."

WISE UP WORDS

• rugged individualism   New Deal

WORK

1 Look at the factfile on Herbert Hoover.
   a What is meant by the phrase 'rugged individual'?
   b Can you think of anything in Hoover's early life that might have led him to believe in 'rugged individualism'?

2 Look at the factfile on FDR.
   a What were the three Rs?
   b Can you think of anything in FDR's early life that might have made people think that he could be a suitable man to lead America out of the Depression?

3 Look at **Source A**. In your own words, explain how this poster tries to get people to vote for the Democratic Party candidate, FDR.

4 Look at **Source B**. What do you think Hoover meant when he said that the 1932 election was 'a contest between two styles of government'? In what ways did the Republican and Democratic parties differ?

5 Look at **Source C**.
   a What does FDR promise the American people?
   b Why do you think voters loved the phrase 'New Deal' so much?
   c In your own words, describe the mood of FDR's speech.

6 Look at **Source E**.
   a What does the writer mean by 'he [FDR] showed that his physical problems were no barrier to him'?
   b According to this source, why was FDR so popular with the voters?

7 Design a campaign poster trying to get people to vote for FDR's Democratic Party. Like all good campaign posters, you need to think about the following. Will your poster:
   • attack the opposition – in this case, Hoover, the Republicans and the way they have dealt with the Depression?
   • concentrate on your candidate – in other words, reasons why FDR would make a good president?
   • emphasise your party's ideas and plans – will your poster mention the New Deal and/or the three Rs?

GCSE Question time

• How far was Roosevelt himself responsible for his election victory in 1932?

• What were Hoover's economic policies?

• How did Roosevelt's early life prepare him for a career in politics?

A 'New Deal'

AIMS ....

Your main aims here are to:
- know three new laws that FDR introduced as soon as he became President;
- work out whether the cartoon on page 71 was drawn by a supporter or an opponent of FDR.

Franklin Delano Roosevelt had promised Americans a New Deal. Now he had to deliver on his promise. He knew he had to devise ways to help millions of people hit hard by years of depression … quickly! In a famous speech made on the day he was sworn in as President, he promised 'action and action now'. He didn't disappoint people. In the first 100 days of FDR's time as President, Americans saw more action being taken to end the Depression than they had seen since it began. And in his first week in charge, FDR made some changes that instantly made Americans realise he meant business!

▼ **_Source A_** *Part of one of FDR's famous **fireside chats**.*

> "I can assure you that it is safer to keep your money in a reopened bank than under the mattress."

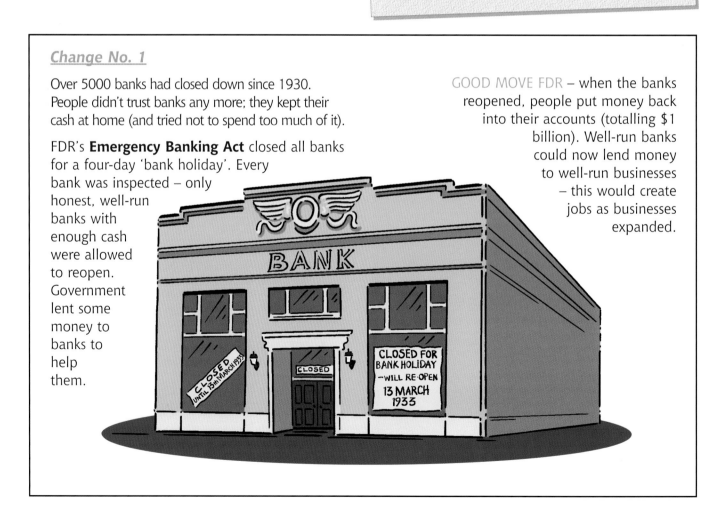

Change No. 1

Over 5000 banks had closed down since 1930. People didn't trust banks any more; they kept their cash at home (and tried not to spend too much of it).

FDR's **Emergency Banking Act** closed all banks for a four-day 'bank holiday'. Every bank was inspected – only honest, well-run banks with enough cash were allowed to reopen. Government lent some money to banks to help them.

GOOD MOVE FDR – when the banks reopened, people put money back into their accounts (totalling $1 billion). Well-run banks could now lend money to well-run businesses – this would create jobs as businesses expanded.

CLOSED UNTIL 13th MARCH 1933

BANK

CLOSED

CLOSED FOR BANK HOLIDAY – WILL RE-OPEN 13 MARCH 1933

Change No. 2

FDR's next move saved money. The **Economy Act** cut the pay of everyone working for the government, the army, the navy and air force by 15%.

GOOD MOVE FDR – he saved nearly a billion dollars, which could now be used to help the unemployed.

Change No. 3

The **Beer Act** made it legal to make and sell alcohol again.

GOOD MOVE FDR – people were fed up with all the problems Prohibition had caused – the gangsters, the killings, the corrupt cops and crooked dealings. And now alcohol was legal, the government could raise money by taxing it!

Change No. 4

FDR used the radio to explain his ideas. He was the first president to do this. His fireside chats, as they were called, were a great novelty for the American people – he even spoke about his family and his pet dog, Fala.

GOOD MOVE FDR – many Americans were convinced that their President was a man who was genuinely 'in touch' with them.

You have nothing to fear … this nation asks for action and action now … put people to work … this problem can be solved …

▼ **Source B** *Actor Ossie Davis remembering an FDR radio speech, featured on the 'Stormy Weather' episode of the TV series* America's Century,

"And me, a little black boy down in Georgia, hearing that voice over the radio, I felt that it wasn't that he told it to Daddy and Daddy told it to me or he told it to Momma and she told it to me – no, he was talking to little Ossie, sitting there listening to him. He could, through the magic of his voice and radio, reach out and involve you in the great adventure of making America work again."

WISE UP WORDS

- Emergency Banking Act   Economy Act   Beer Act   fireside chats   contemporary   lame duck months

FACT   *New President, new powers*

FDR, an experienced politician, knew that ideas and proposals usually took years to become law because politicians argued about things so much. To overcome this, he asked Congress, the American parliament, to give him extra powers to introduce laws quickly … and agree with everything he did! Amazingly, Congress went along with the idea and for one hundred days (8 March–6 June 1933), they gave him the same powers as if the country were being invaded.

FACT   *'Lame duck'*

FDR won the election in November 1932. But the American Constitution states that a losing president is allowed four months to finish off their work – so FDR couldn't start his job until March 1933! These are often known as **lame duck months.** Hoover used this time to spend money – he gave out loans to businesses in trouble for example. But the Depression got even worse during the lame duck months as unemployment rose and more banks closed. Whilst FDR waited impatiently to begin his Presidency, he accused Hoover of 'reckless and extravagant spending'. FDR finally started work on Saturday 4 March 1933.

▶ This cartoon appeared in an American newspaper in March 1933. The ability to analyse **contemporary** cartoons is a valuable skill. Study the cartoon. Think carefully about the message the cartoonist was trying to put across.

What building is this and why is HH leaving it?

'Commission form of Government' refers to the way that any new idea has to be discussed for many months by different groups or commissions before becoming law. Why is this shown in the dustbin?

What does it usually mean if you 'pull your sleeves up'?

Who is this and why do you think the cartoonist has drawn him smiling?

'GOP' stands for Grand Old Party, the nickname given to the Republican Party. Why is FDR throwing out GOP policies (ideas and plans)?

Who is HH?

Explain what each piece of rubbish means. Why is FDR throwing it out?

WORK

1

Name of Act	What did it do?	Why did it make FDR popular?	How did it help America recover?
Emergency Banking Act	All banks were closed for...	It made Americans realise that the government was actually going to do something to help...	If the banks had money they would be able...
Economy Act			
Beer Act			

Copy out and complete the chart (above) based around three of FDR's key changes soon after becoming President. The first one has been partially done for you.

2 a Why do you think FDR's 'fireside chats' were a good idea?

  b With so much work to do, why did FDR bother to tell people about his family and his dog?

3 Look carefully at the cartoon above. It appeared just after FDR started his presidency in 1933.

  a In rough, answer each of the questions surrounding the cartoon.

  b Complete the following question in detail. What is the message of the cartoon? Explain your answer, referring to details in the cartoon.

GCSE Question time

• Describe the main features of Roosevelt's first 'Hundred Days'.

• Explain why Roosevelt introduced the New Deal.

What were the 'alphabet agencies'?

AIMS ....

The names of the various alphabet agencies are very difficult to learn. Aim to be able to give one example of the way FDR helped: i) people most in need ii) farmers iii) industry iv) the unemployed.

FDR didn't have a fixed plan about how to deal with the Depression when he became President. He surrounded himself with clever men and women with fresh ideas and gave them encouragement. He called them his **Brain Trust**. Sometimes their new ideas worked, sometimes they didn't. On occasions, some ideas clashed with others, but, on the whole, the American public were pleased to see their new President *trying* to help them to overcome their problems.

FDR's new ideas, measures and laws soon picked up a nickname – they were called **alphabet agencies** because the various organisations that provided a service were known by their initials.

HELP FOR THOSE IN NEED

HOLC (Home Owners Loan Corporation)

Government loaned money at very low rates of interest to people who couldn't keep up with their mortgage payments. 300 000 homeowners helped in the first year.

FERA (Federal Emergency Relief Agency)

$500 million given to states to help homeless, starving people. Money spent on soup kitchens, blankets, clothes and nursery schools (so parents could go out to find a job in the day).

FERA
SOUP AND BLANKETS HERE

▼ **_Source A_** *From the TV documentary* America's Century.

"Most people weren't sure what he meant when he promised a New Deal to the American people – neither was he! But Roosevelt appeared optimistic, confident ... and he wasn't Herbert Hoover!"

Native American Indians

FDR was one of the first presidents to encourage Native American Indians to *increase* the amount of land they owned. Government loans were provided to buy more land, set up businesses and buy farming equipment. The Indian Reservation Act of 1934 gave Native Americans the right to manage their own affairs, such as setting up their own law courts. However, many Native Americans still lived in great poverty and suffered from prejudice and discrimination.

HELP FOR INDUSTRY AND WORKERS

NRA (National Recovery Administration)

The NRA encouraged workers and employers to get together to work out a code of fair conditions. Any business or factory that guaranteed a decent wage, improved working conditions and set a limit on hours of work per week was allowed to use the symbol of the NRA – a blue eagle – to help advertise its products.

Buyers of a 'blue eagle product' could tell it had been made to a good standard under decent conditions. It also stated that workers should have the right to join a trade union, something that had been banned in some industries.

▼ **Source B** *By September 1933, over 500 industries, ranging from cotton factories to car makers, had signed NRA codes. This covered nearly 22 million workers and two million employers. Big publicity campaigns, posters, parades and even beauty pageants encouraged members of the public to buy from companies that had signed the NRA code.*

HELP FOR FARMERS

FCA (Farm Credit Administration)

Loans to farmers who were unable to meet their mortgage payments. $100 million loaned out in 18 months.

AAA (Agricultural Adjustment Agency)

By the end of the 1920s, farmers had been producing too much food. As a result, prices for wheat, oats, barley, tobacco and cotton had fallen (if there is a lot of something, a farmer can't ask a high price). The AAA paid farmers to produce *less* and destroy some of the food they had already produced! They hoped that food prices would rise because it was in short supply (if there is less of something, a farmer can ask for more money). The idea worked – between 1933 and 1939, farmers' incomes doubled. However, the government was heavily criticised for this idea – the government was destroying food and forcing up prices to help farmers at a time when millions in the cities were going hungry.

FOOD PRICES

HELP FOR THE UNEMPLOYED

CCC (Civilian Conservation Corps)

Unemployed 18- to 25-year-olds were given food and shelter in the countryside. For one dollar a day, they did conservation work – planted trees, dug canals, stocked rivers with fish, cleared footpaths and strengthened river banks against flooding. They started a programme to control mosquitoes – and ended malaria in America. Some money was sent home to their families too. CCC created jobs for 2.5 million men.

PWA (Public Works Administration)

The PWA gave funds of $3300 million. Money was spent buying materials and employing millions of skilled workers to build schools, housing, hospitals, bridges, courtrooms and dams. The PWA also built ten ships and fifty airports.

▲ **Source C** *The PWA builds a school, 1935.*

CWA (Civil Works Administration)

The CWA provided temporary work for four million men, building schools, airports, roads and even 150 000 public toilets! The CWA changed its name to WPA (Workers Progress Administration) in 1935. They didn't just provide work for skilled builders and architects, but also:

* unemployed actors were hired to give free shows;
* artists were hired to paint pictures for display in schools;
* people were hired to carry balloons around Washington to scare pigeons away from important historic buildings;
* out of work researchers were even paid to write a book on the history of the safety pin!

When the man in charge of the schemes, Harry Hopkins, was criticised for wasting taxpayers' money, he said, 'Hell, they've got to eat just like the rest of us!' By 1941, the CWA and WPA had spent $11 000 million and provided work for eight million people.

FDR's theory behind many of his alphabet agencies was simple – the government creates jobs by *spending* money; once the workers earn wages, they start buying goods. Firms and businesses then start hiring new workers; these new workers spend money and so on. Some people used the phrase **priming the pump** to describe this idea (see **Source D**).

▼ **Source D** *FDR's idea of priming the pump was influenced by an Englishman, J M Keynes, who said that governments should spend money in times of depression to get the economy going again.*

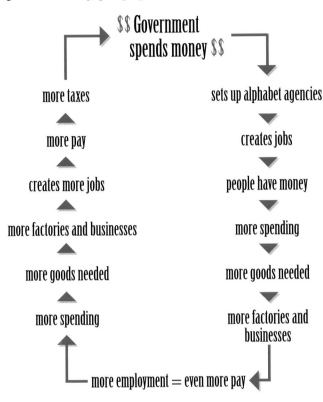

$$\text{Government spends money}$$

more taxes

more pay

creates more jobs

more factories and businesses

more goods needed

more spending

more employment = even more pay

sets up alphabet agencies

creates jobs

people have money

more spending

more goods needed

more factories and businesses

▼ **Source E** *From a New Jersey factory noticeboard, 1933.*

FACTORY NOTICE

President Roosevelt has done his part; now you do something. Buy something – buy anything...

Paint your kitchen
Send a telegram
Give a party
Get a car
Pay a bill
Rent a flat
Fix your roof
Get a haircut
See a show
Build a house
Take a trip
Get married

It doesn't matter what you do – but get going and keep going. This country is starting to move.

▼ **Source F** *From the hit 2003 film Seabiscuit, a true story about a famous American racehorse from the 1930s.*

"They call it 'relief' but it was a lot more than that. It had dozens of names — NRA, WPA, the CCC — but it really came down to just one thing. For the first time in a long time, someone cared. For the first time in a long time, you were no longer alone."

WISE UP WORDS

- Brain Trust   alphabet agencies
  'priming the pump'

WORK

1 **a** What steps did FDR take to help i) the homeless ii) homeowners iii) farmers iv) industry v) the unemployed?

   b FDR once said that hungry and unemployed people 'are the stuff that revolutions are made of'. What do you think he meant by this?

2 **a** Why do you think the AAA was one of FDR's most criticised agencies?

   b How do you think FDR and his advisors justified the AAA?

3 Look at **Source C**.

   a Which 'alphabet agency' is building this school?

   b How can you tell from this photograph that this was one of thousands of work projects started by this agency?

   c What sort of jobs did this project create? List as many as you can, even using the sign in the photograph to help you.

4 What did FDR mean when he said he was 'priming the pump' of America's economy?

5 Pick any of FDR's alphabet agencies. Put together a 'fireside chat' to be given by FDR over the radio. In it, you will have to explain what it is, whom it is targeting and what it is hoped it will achieve. Your 'chat' should last no longer than one minute.

'We have an opportunity here': how successful was the TVA?

AIMS

Aim to understand:
- What changes the TVA made to the Tennessee Valley;
- Why the TVA was seen as 'the pride of FDR's New Deal'.

In January 1933, FDR visited an area of America called the Tennessee Valley. He was so shocked by what he saw that he called the area 'our nation's number one problem'. Within weeks, he set up a special alphabet agency – the Tennessee Valley Authority (TVA) – to help those who lived there.

So what was so bad about the Tennessee Valley? Why did this area get special treatment? And how well did the TVA perform?

The Tennessee Valley is the area of land around the Tennessee River. It covers an area the size of England and Wales put together and stretches over seven states (see **Source A**). It was, without doubt, one of the poorest parts of the country:

- The Tennessee River flooded every spring, washing away millions of tons of soil and destroying many farms. The river dried out in the summer and high winds blew away even more soil.
- Only three out of every one hundred farms had electricity.
- Half of the three million people living in the valley relied on charity donations.
- There were hardly any factory jobs.
- Levels of vitamin deficiency and disease were amongst the highest in the country.

FDR saw this area as an ideal place for one of his New Deal alphabet agencies and set up the TVA in May 1933 (see **Source B**).

▼ **Source A** *A map showing parts of the USA covered by the TVA (80 000 square miles).*

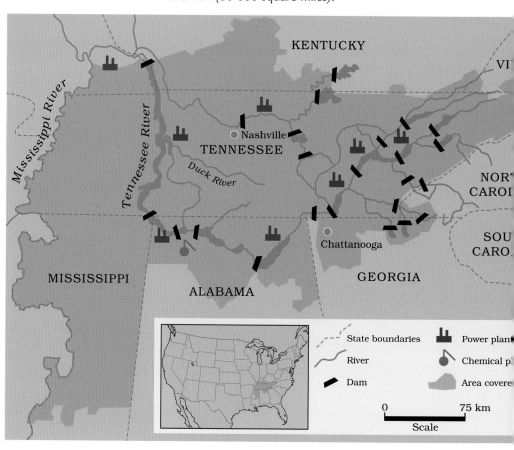

Source B *A speech made by FDR shortly after visiting Muscle Shoals, a town within the Tennessee Valley.*

"We have an opportunity here to set an example of planning for generations to come. We have the opportunity to tie industry, agriculture, forestry and flood prevention together in one agency that covers a thousand miles. We can make better opportunities and a better place to live for millions of people."

It didn't take the man in charge of the TVA long to realise that most of the area's problems were directly linked to the Tennessee River. To control it, they built over 20 dams. At the touch of a button, dam managers could close huge gates whenever the river threatened to flood. These dams had many benefits:

- They provided cheap electricity, created when powerful turbines built into the walls of each new dam were spun round by jets of water released from the lakes behind them. By 1940, the TVA was America's biggest producer of electricity.

- Cheap electricity attracted factories to the area – car makers, paper mills, steel makers, food factories and fertiliser producers all created jobs.

- The dams meant the river was much calmer, ideal for water transport. 650 miles of river could now be used by ships to take coal, steel and other goods to and from the factories.

- The dams controlled flooding, which meant that farms could perform better and grow more crops. By 1950, 93% of farms were hooked up to an electricity supply.

- Now the flow of the water had been controlled, it became easier to control killer diseases like malaria (spread by mosquitoes, an insect that thrives in wet areas).

- The lakes created behind the dams produced a new holiday area. New housing and water sports facilities were built alongside the lakes.

The TVA was one of the most impressive alphabet agencies. The Tennessee River was tamed, thousands of jobs were created, the land was conserved and the health and well-being of an entire region improved. To many, the TVA was the pride of FDR's New Deal.

Source C *The Norris Dam, built by the TVA between 1933 and 1936.*

Source D *The words of Lorena Hickok, interviewed in 1934. From BBC series* American Voices, *2000.*

"What's happening there – it's like a promised land. The Tennessee Valley was about the poorest region in the nation but go there now and you'll see thousands of men building in timber and steel and concrete. I didn't know much about it before I went but I spent a week driving around. I saw the Norris Dam ... the Wilson Dam and the foundations of the Wheeler Dam ... the whole thing was so exciting ... it's as if TVA is more than a federal agency, it's an empire and its potential is so extraordinary that it makes me gasp – decent housing, decent wages, a new kind of life – and all because the government is in control. I mean, gosh, what possibilities!"

WORK

1. Why do you think FDR called the Tennessee Valley 'our nation's number one problem'?

2. Look at **Source A.**
   a. How many states were affected by the work of the TVA? List them.
   b. How many dams did the TVA build?
   c. List four ways in which the TVA dams helped to improve the Tennessee Valley.

3. Look at **Source D.**
   a. Why was Lorena Hickok so impressed by the TVA?
   b. Do you think the TVA deserves its label as 'the pride of the New Deal'? Give reasons for your answer.

The New Deal under attack

AIMS

Aim to remember at least three reasons why people opposed FDR and his New Deal.

Not everyone liked FDR's New Deal. Some thought it interfered too much in the lives of ordinary Americans, whilst others believed it didn't help people enough.

The rich

To help pay for the New Deal, FDR made rich people pay more tax. Not surprisingly, they didn't like this! They resented the way some of FDR's alphabet agencies paid people to plant trees, paint pictures and stock rivers with fish – they said this was a waste of money.

Source A *An American cartoon called 'Priming the Pump', from 1933. In your opinion, what is the cartoonist saying is wrong with the New Deal?*

Source B *A rich American businessman's opinion of the New Deal.*

"The President was a rich man's son and he betrayed his own class. He wasted billions of dollars on his schemes. He didn't understand that when you give to people you hurt them. We had soup lines and the Depression because people lost confidence in themselves. Welfare [help given to people in need] kills a man's spirit because it makes him lose the will to fend for himself. If you want a dog to hunt, you have to let him go hungry. If you want a man to be successful, he needs to face the setbacks of life."

Businessmen

Many businessmen, especially wealthy ones, didn't like the way the New Deal 'interfered' with business and gave more rights to workers. The NRA codes, for example, were criticised by company bosses because they allowed workers to join trade unions and forced employers to pay minimum wages, improve working conditions and set limits on hours of work. Whilst workers benefited from the NRA codes, some businessmen didn't like them because they had to pay for the changes!

Supreme Court

The **Supreme Court** is America's highest court. Consisting of nine top judges, its job is to make sure that any new laws are legal and do not go against America's strict Constitution. There are many parts to America's Constitution but one of them outlines

WISE UP WORD

- Supreme Court

the role of the president. The rules state that he or she is only responsible for national affairs affecting <u>all</u> states. State governments are responsible for all other affairs. So, for example, the president – or *federal* government as it is known – makes decisions on issues which affect the whole country (like wars and taxes) whilst the *state* governments deal with things that affect their own state, like whether to have the death penalty or not. In 1935, the Supreme Court ruled that one of FDR's alphabet agencies, the AAA, was illegal. They said that giving help to farmers was a matter for *state* governments, not the *federal* government. As a result, all the help that the AAA gave to farmers stopped!

The Supreme Court also declared many of the NRA codes illegal. They ruled that the federal government had no right to improve rules on business – it was up to state governments to do it.

Source C *A British cartoon from* Punch *magazine on the quarrel between FDR and the Supreme Court. The cartoon is called 'The Illegal Act'. What point do you think the cartoonist is trying to make?*

THE ILLEGAL ACT.

PRESIDENT ROOSEVELT. "I'M SORRY, BUT THE SUPREME COURT SAYS I MUST CHUCK YOU BACK AGAIN."

Republicans

Millions of people still supported the Republican Party. Many were 'rugged individuals' too, believing that people should be left to live their own lives and sort out their own problems. Many Republicans were horrified by the way this huge government-run scheme – the New Deal – was dominating people's lives. Some said that Roosevelt was behaving like a dictator and making the government too powerful. Others claimed that all this government help would make Americans 'soft' and 'unable to stand on their own two feet'. Some even worried that America would soon be controlled by the government … and this was the type of system that Communist Russia had!

Other ideas for a New Deal

- Huey Long, a popular politician from Louisiana, suggested an alternative for the New Deal called 'Share Our Wealth' – he said if he were president, all fortunes over $5 million would be confiscated and shared out. He also promised every American family $5000 to buy a radio, a car and a house as well as cheap food for the poor, houses for war veterans, free education and a minimum wage. He may have run for president in 1936 but was shot dead in 1935 by a young doctor whose reputation he had ruined.

- Francis Townsend, a retired doctor from California, wanted everyone to retire at 60 to give more job opportunities for younger people.

- Charles Coughlin set up the National Union for Social Justice. Its aim was to provide work and fair wages for everyone. However, he made speeches attacking Jews and trade unions and his support declined.

WORK

1 Look at **Sources A** and **C**. For each cartoon:
   a Explain the point the cartoonist was trying to make.
   b Decide whether the cartoonist in each was for or against FDR and the New Deal.

2 Look at **Source B**.
   a What do you think the writer means when he says FDR has 'betrayed his own class'?
   b Why does the writer criticise 'welfare'?

How was the Second New Deal different from the First?

By 1935, both FDR and the New Deal were being criticised. Some said change didn't come quickly enough whilst others thought FDR had become 'power mad'. The Supreme Court even banned two of his alphabet agencies – the NRA and the AAA – when they were ruled 'illegal and unconstitutional'. Despite this, FDR still thought there was a lot of work to be done. He still wanted to change aspects of American society he felt were unfair and improve things for ordinary people. FDR's next phase of plans are often called the 'Second New Deal'.

NLRA (National Labour Relations Act)

Workers were allowed to join trade unions so they could campaign for better pay and conditions. In the past, some employers, like Henry Ford, had sacked workers who had formed groups or unions. Now it was hoped that bosses would have to listen if their workforce was unhappy. The NRLA was seen as a replacement for the scrapped NRA.

SSA (Social Security Act)

Government pensions were provided for old people, widows and disabled people. The SSA also established a system of payments for the sick and unemployed.

FSA (Farm Security Administration)

Government loans were given to tenant farmers (people who rented land from a large landowner) so they could buy their own land. The FSA also set up clean, healthy camps to help poor farming families who had lost their own farms or left them to find work around the country.

SCA (Soil Conservation Agency)

Money was given to farmers who conserved and improved the soil on their farms. The SCA was seen as a replacement for the AAA.

FACT *Bad move Mr President*

In 1935, the nine judges of the Supreme Court – America's highest Court – had declared a few of FDR's alphabet agencies illegal. They ruled that the AAA and the NRA were 'unlawful' because the President had no right to give help to farmers or interfere in business – this, they argued, was the role of individual state governments, *not* the federal government.

FDR hit back and tried to increase the number of judges in the Supreme Court. He claimed that the nine existing judges were too old to cope with all the work he was giving them. By putting in extra 'new' judges (who liked FDR's New Deal), he hoped his men could 'outvote' the nine if they tried to block his ideas.

FDR's idea was very unpopular. Many people accused him of wanting to rule America as a dictator. At a time when Adolf Hitler was making headlines for the way he was ruling Germany, FDR decided to scrap his plans. However, never again did the Supreme Court block one of FDR's New Deal proposals!

In November 1936, FDR faced his second election. Voters had the chance to show whether they supported his New Deal or not. The Republican Party chose a very popular politician, Alf London, to run against FDR. In speeches, London openly criticised FDR, calling his New Deal a waste of taxpayers' money. He outlined different sections of

American society who he felt hadn't benefited in FDR's time as President. But his efforts had no effect. FDR won easily, receiving more votes than any other president in American history. In a speech soon after his victory, FDR joked, 'It seems everyone is against the New Deal ... except the voters!'

▼ **Source A** *An American cartoon of the 1936 presidential election. In only two states, Vermont and Maine, did FDR's Democratic Party not win more votes than the Republicans.*

WORK

1 Write a sentence or two to explain each of the following: • SSA • NLRA • FSA • SCA

2 **a** In your opinion, briefly explain why FDR had to scrap several of his alphabet agencies and introduce a Second New Deal.

 b Why did FDR plan to appoint his supporters as extra new judges on the Supreme Court?

 c Why do you think this move alarmed many Americans?

3 Look at **Source A**.

 a What is meant by the phrase 'in the dog house'?

 b Why are Vermont and Maine 'in the dog house'?

 c Do you think the cartoonist supported or opposed FDR and the New Deal? Give reasons for your answer.

4 What did FDR mean when he said, 'it seems everyone is against the New Deal ... except the voters'?

The end of the New Deal

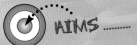

AIMS ....

Over the next four pages, aim to understand:

- why unemployment levels began to increase after 1937;
- how America became involved in the Second World War;
- what effect the war had on the American economy.

When FDR was re-elected as President in November 1936, he still believed he had lots of work to do (see **Source A**). But he was getting more and more worried by the amount of money being spent on his job creation schemes and projects, like the WPA and TVA. In response, he decided to cut down the amount spent on his New Deal programmes – but this created a problem. Unemployment jumped by three million because the government was no longer providing people with so many jobs. At the same time, thousands of workers in the car and steel industries went on strike as part of the campaign for better wages and conditions.

By 1938, some people were commenting that America was 'sliding downhill' towards depression again. Unemployment went back up to 10.5 million and car and steel production was falling month after month. Even FDR himself acknowledged that the New Deal had come to an end by January 1939. But events in Europe were about to provide a dramatic solution to some of America's problems.

▼ **_Source A_** _FDR speaking after his election in 1936._

> "Of course we will continue to improve working conditions for the workers of America … of course we will continue to work for cheap electricity in our homes and on farms … of course we will continue our efforts on behalf of farmers … of course we will continue our efforts for young men and women, for crippled, blind, unemployed, elderly … of course we will continue to protect the consumer."

America and the Second World War

America had kept out of the affairs of other countries for several years. They called it **isolationism**. In 1934, the **Johnson Act** banned loans to countries involved in wars and two **Neutrality Laws** were passed in 1935 and 1937 to keep America out of any conflict abroad. But when the Second World War began in September 1939, America supported Britain and France against Hitler's Germany and their allies. FDR feared that if Germany defeated Britain and France, then America may come under attack soon after. The President didn't send American soldiers to actually fight against the Nazis – instead he was prepared to sell top-quality, American-made weapons to Britain and France – if they wanted them. Both nations were eager to buy!

- The **Cash and Carry Plan**: In November 1939, Britain and France began buying weapons, warships and planes from America. This created valuable jobs at a time when unemployment was rising. However, in June 1940, Germany attacked and defeated France. Britain stood alone as Hitler's armies began invading most of the major European countries. When the British government ran short of money, FDR _gave_ them 50 warships … and began thinking of another way to support the British.

- **Lend-Lease**: In March 1941, when Britain was desperately short of money, FDR agreed to a 'Lend-Lease' deal. Instead of selling, America would 'lend' Britain up to $7000 million worth of weapons. Most people knew that America would never get, or want, them back! They struck a similar deal with Russia when Germany attacked them in June 1941.

Despite their official position of **neutrality**, it was clear that America supported Britain's war against Hitler's Germany. However, not all Americans were pleased with events. Organisations such as 'The Mother's Crusade' and the 'America First Committee' had big, public anti-war demonstrations because they feared America might get dragged into a European war. But others soon began to see the benefits of an end to isolationism. As America began to rearm in case they were forced to enter the war, millions found jobs building fighter planes, battleships and tanks. Unemployed men became trainee soldiers, sailors and pilots. When the American people voted FDR in as President AGAIN in 1940, unemployment was starting to drop. In 1941, there were just 5.5 million unemployed compared to over 10 million just four years before. To some, it seemed as if World War Two, and not FDR's New Deal, was now beginning to get Americans back to work.

▼ **Source B** *Chrysler, the car makers, began making tanks in the late 1930s. This photograph shows tanks on their assembly line. In total, America produced 297 000 fighter and bomber planes, 86 000 tanks and 12 000 ships between 1939 and 1945.*

▼ **Source C** *Raymond Moley, a former member of FDR's government, writing in 1945.*

"After 1936, our economy began to slide downhill and our employment increased … it was the war that saved the economy and saved Roosevelt."

WORK

Look at **Source A**.

1 a Which five-word phrase does FDR repeat FIVE times during his speech?

   b Why do you think he chose to repeat this phrase so many times?

   c Why do you think FDR identified so many problems in America even though he had been President for four years by 1936?

2 Why did unemployment levels start to rise after 1937?

3 Write a sentence or two about each of the following:
   • isolationism   • neutrality
   • the Cash and Carry Plan   • Lend-Lease
   • the Mothers' Crusade

4 Look at **Source C**.

   a Raymond Moley was sacked by FDR in 1936. Could this explain why he was not a supporter of FDR? Explain your answer.

   b Does the bias in this source mean it is of no value to historians?

5 In the Presidential election of 1940, these two slogans appeared on campaign posters. One was used by FDR's Democratic Party, the other by the Republicans.

   'No man is good three times.'

   'Better to be a third-timer than a third-rater.'

   a Which do you think was the Democratic Party slogan and which was used by the Republicans? Explain your choice.

   b In your own words, explain what each slogan means.

'December 7, 1941 – a date which will live in infamy'

America officially entered World War Two in December 1941. After several years of supporting Britain and her allies by selling and loaning them weapons, FDR and Congress finally made the decision to send men to fight. So why did America join in? What had happened on 7 December to make America suddenly end many years of neutrality?

The roots of America's entry into World War Two lie in their relationship with Japan. During the 1930s, Japan began to invade many of the countries surrounding them, including China. Japan, a relatively small country with a large population, wanted to get their hands on the food and raw materials that these nations produced – rice, coal, tin, rubber and oil. In protest at Japan's aggression, FDR vowed not to sell any oil or steel to Japan. The Japanese weren't happy; their industries used millions of tons of US steel and oil every year!

As the relationship between the two countries grew worse and worse, Japanese military leaders planned a secret and surprise attack on US ships at a naval base in the Hawaiian Islands called Pearl Harbor. It was from here that American battleships would attack Japan if ever war broke out.

The Japanese thought that if they destroyed enough ships, the Americans would be unable to stop them from taking all the territory they wanted. By the time the Americans rebuilt their navy, the Japanese would be too strong and have enough food and raw materials to ever be removed from any of the countries they had invaded.

At 7:55am on Sunday 7 December 1941, 183 Japanese bomber planes attacked the American navy at its base at Pearl Harbor. The Americans were caught completely by surprise. In just under two hours, 21 US warships were sunk or damaged, 177 US planes were destroyed and over 2000 men were killed. The Japanese lost just 29 planes.

The next day, America and Britain declared war on Japan. Three days later, Germany and Italy, Japan's official allies, declared war on America. Now the world's richest, most powerful country was involved in what was to become the world's most expensive, most destructive and most famous war.

▼ **Source D** *A speech made by FDR on 8 December 1941.*

"Yesterday, December 7, 1941 – a date which will live in infamy – the USA was suddenly and deliberately attacked by naval and air forces of the Empire of Japan … the attack on the Hawaiian Islands has caused severe damage … I regret to tell you that very many American lives have been lost.

Yesterday the Japanese also launched attacks against Malaya … Hong Kong … Guam … the Philippines … Wake Island … and Midway Island….

No matter how long it may take us to overcome this invasion, the American people will win through to absolute victory."

WISE UP WORDS

- isolationism neutrality Johnson Act Neutrality Laws Cash and Carry Plan Lend-Lease

Source E *A still from the 2001 Hollywood film* Pearl Harbor.

Source F *A photograph of one of the American planes destroyed during the attack, taken on 8 December, 1941.*

Source G *A newspaper headline from 8 December 1941.*

NEW YORK TIMES

Monday 8 December 1941

1500 DEAD IN HAWAII

CONGRESS VOTES WAR

FACT *Not such a great success!*

Despite terrible losses, the attack could have been much worse for the Americans. Part of their navy, including the aircraft carriers, was out at sea when the attack took place. They escaped undamaged. It would not take as long as the Japanese hoped for the American navy to get back to full strength.

Source H *A modern historian sums up how the war helped to end the Depression.*

"For the next four years, 1941 to 1945, American soldiers, sailors and airmen fought in Europe, North Africa and the Pacific. In all, 7.2 million American servicemen fought in the Second World War. To keep this enormous army supplied with weapons and equipment, American industry had to boost its output massively. New factories were built and … people who had been unemployed throughout the Depression now found it easy to get work."

WORK

1 **a** Why did relations between America and Japan get worse and worse during the 1930s?

   b Why did Japan choose to attack Pearl Harbor?

2 **a** Remind yourself what isolationism means.

   b Did America abandon isolationism when they declared war after the Japanese attack on Pearl Harbor – or had it already done so before this?

3 How did World War Two help FDR solve some of America's economic problems? Suggest as many reasons as you can. You might wish to use **Sources B** and **H** to help you.

4 Write a front-page news story for 8 December 1941. Remember to include: • a 'catchy' headline • FDR's response • facts and figures • a picture • your thoughts on the future of the conflict.

FDR and the New Deal: success or failure?

AIMS ....

In this final section, aim to form your own opinion on FDR and his New Deal - was it a success or not?

At around 1:00pm on 12 April 1945, whilst having his portrait painted, FDR complained of a severe headache and fainted. He died two hours later of a stroke, without regaining consciousness.

Most of America's presidents had served one or maybe two four-year terms of office. But FDR was unique. He remains the only president to be elected four times – 1932, 1936, 1940 and 1944! Understandably, many Americans today regard FDR as one of their greatest presidents because of his efforts during the Depression and his world famous New Deal. But is his reputation deserved? Did the New Deal work ... or is FDR's image as the saviour of the American economy undeserved?

Study **Sources A** to **L** carefully. Some were created by people living at the time of the New Deal whilst others were written later by historians. Whilst analysing the sources, try to think about each of these key questions:

- Did the New Deal help all those people hit hard by the Depression?
- Did the New Deal revive American business and help the economy to recover?
- Did the New Deal help to build a better America?

▼ **Source A** *A modern historian, writing in 1996.*

"FDR gave the federal government a job to do: to look after the weaker members of society — the old, the ill, the unemployed, the poor — and to build a better country. That was a vision of their country which many young Americans could accept."

▼ **Source B** *A letter sent to the White House in 1934. Which alphabet agency do you think helped this couple? Two other envelopes sent to FDR had these addresses: 'God's gift to the USA, the White House, Washington' and 'To the Greatest Man in the World, the White House'.*

'Dear Mr President,

This is just to tell you everything is all right now. The man you sent found our house and we went to the bank with him. Our mortgage can go on a while longer. You remember I wrote about losing the furniture too. Well, your man got that back for us. I never heard of a President like you, Mr Roosevelt. My wife and I are old and don't amount to much but we join with millions of others in praying for you every night. God bless you, Mr Roosevelt...'

▼ **Source C** *A copy of a cartoon from 1933 called 'Yes, you remembered me'. Is this a cartoon for or against FDR's New Deal? Give reasons for your decision.*

▼ **Source D** *Unemployment in the USA, 1929–1945.*

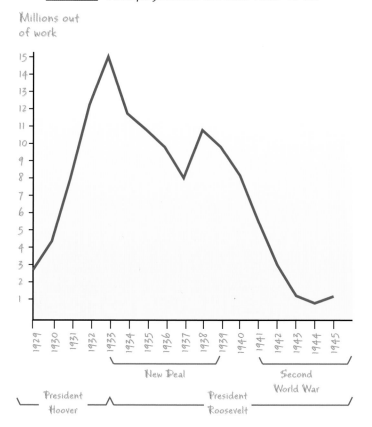

▼ **Source E** *A modern historian's opinion of FDR's New Deal.*

"Roosevelt was a practical man, not a brilliant thinker. His answers to different problems could lead to conflicts. For example, higher food prices helped farmers but hit the poor. Cutting spending to balance the budget led to more unemployment. Blue Eagle codes might protect the consumer, but they made business less profitable. For some people, he didn't go far enough: unemployment remained · high, poverty was still common, big businesses were still powerful."

▼ **Source F** *Number of bank failures, 1920–1941. Note that FDR became president in 1932, but didn't start work until 1933.*

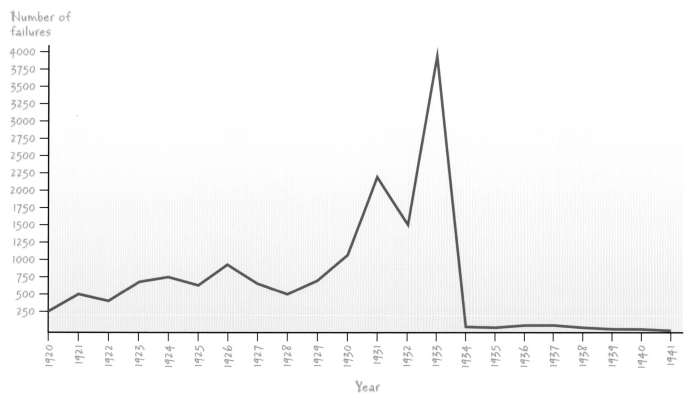

▼ **Source G** *Days lost in strikes 1930–1938. The chart shows the number of workers on strike over a number of days. For example, 1000 workers on strike for ten days would mean 10 000 days 'lost on strikes'. The figures are often used to show how satisfied workers are with their pay and conditions – the less time lost on strikes, the happier the workers are and vice versa.*

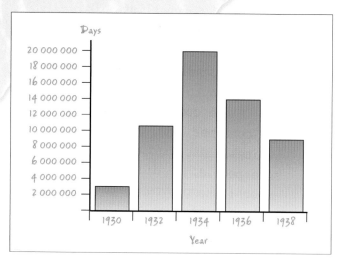

▼ **Source H** *A modern historian commenting on the effects of the New Deal on Black Americans.*

" [During the New Deal] blacks remained second-class citizens. There was still widespread racism and discrimination … blacks were out in segregated CCC camps and when the new town of Norris was built in the Tennessee Valley, blacks were not allowed to live there…. Black people found it hard to get work … jobs were usually given to whites and the jobs that the blacks did get were often menial [basic] ones… [However,] thousands received much more relief [aid] than ever before. Around 200 000 blacks benefited from the CCC…"

▼ **Source I** *A modern historian commenting on the effect of the New Deal on women.*

"The New Deal offered little to women. [One Act] of 1933 drew up a series of codes which set minimum wages, prices and maximum working hours in industry. About a quarter of these codes actually required women to be paid less than men. Only 8000 women were employed by the CCC out of the 2.75 million involved in the scheme … the average pay for a woman in 1937 was $525 compared to $1027 for a man. The situation for black women was worse: 40% of black women worked, but for even lower wages than white women."

▼ **Source J** *From a modern school history textbook.*

"Although it did much to help the forgotten men of America, it [the New Deal] did not end the Depression. It would take another world war to bring back full employment to America."

Source K *From historian C P Hill in his book* Franklin Roosevelt, 1966.

"What did the New Deal achieve? … It certainly did not cure the Depression. And many have maintained that it did not even do much to help American business recover … yet it had notable achievements to its credit … the transformation of the Tennessee Valley under the TVA … the PWA built schools and sewage plants, hospitals, railway stations, bridges and so on … the WPA also gave work to writers, painters, sculptors and actors. But far more significant was the simple fact that the New Deal restored hope to millions of men and women, by providing them with a job or saving their home."

Source L *Written by historian Kenneth C Davis in his book* Don't know much about history. *'Legislative' refers to things FDR did to change the laws of America.*

"But Roosevelt's greatest contribution may have been psychological rather than simply legislative. He possessed a natural gift for restoring confidence, rebuilding optimism and creating hope where all seemed to have been lost … his 'fireside chats' over the radio gave listeners the impression that Roosevelt was sitting in their living rooms speaking to them personally."

WORK

1 Study each source (**A** to **L**) carefully. For each one, you must decide whether it *supports* the view that the New Deal was a success … or whether it *criticises* the New Deal (or both).

Make a copy of the chart below to help you organise this task. The first entry has been done for you, although there are other things you could say about **Source A**!

Source	For (supports) or against (opposes) the New Deal	Explanation (how did you decide?)
A	For – it supports the work of FDR and the New Deal.	The historian writes that the New Deal looked after those people hit hardest by the Depression. This was one of the New Deal's key aims!
B	↓	↓

Remember: some of the sources might not fully support the New Deal or criticise it – they might be a bit of each!

2 Do one of the following tasks.

Either Look at the two views below:

View 1 'FDR was a hero. His New Deal cured the Depression and brought back prosperity.'

View 2 'The New Deal was a waste of taxpayers' money. It didn't actually achieve much at all.'

Each of these views would be heard today if you travelled to America and asked the question, 'The New Deal – was it a success or a failure?'

You must decide which view you agree with most. Use **Sources A** to **L**, and your own knowledge, to support (back up) your viewpoint.

Or

FDR died in April 1945. Write an obituary for him. It should be written from the viewpoint of one of the following:

i) a supporter of FDR who always voted for him and who has benefited from his New Deal; or

ii) an opponent of FDR who thinks that the New Deal was a waste of money and that the war, and not FDR, got America out of the Depression; or

iii) a person who supports FDR because they think his New Deal was a good thing for the American people, but thinks that some of his measures had weaknesses.

Have <u>you</u> been learning?

TASK 1: A NATION'S SAVIOUR?

This cartoon appeared in an American national newspaper in June 1934.

a Who is the man in the cartoon? Write down five facts about him.

b What is the man in the cartoon doing? Why do you think the cartoonist has drawn him sweating a lot?

c What do you think the seeds falling from his hand represent?

d Why do you think the cartoonist has drawn dark clouds in the background?

e Why do you think the cartoonist has drawn the man in white AND with his sleeves rolled up?

f Do you think the cartoonist supports or dislikes the work of the man? Give reasons for your answer.

TASK 2: WHO SAID THAT?

Of all the characters and people you have learned about in this book, who (or what sort of person) is most likely to have said each of the following statements? Write a sentence or two to explain the choices you have made.

a 'We live in constant fear down here ... but it's the lynching that worries us most.'

b 'America is my land of opportunity. I have heard that the streets are paved with gold.'

c 'My hair is short, my skirt is shorter and my morals are low.'

d 'My factory produces a car every ten seconds.'

e 'Some people call me the flying fool.'

f 'KIGY, SANBOG.'

g 'People are always gonna drink – I just give 'em what they want.'

h 'Prosperity is just around the corner.'

i 'I pledge myself to a New Deal for the American people.'

j 'I've lost everything, wiped out in days.'

k 'I hate him, he is wasting my hard-earned tax dollars on more ridiculous alphabet agencies.'

l 'I won the British Golf Open in 1926, 1927 and 1930 and the US Open in 1923, 1926, 1929 and 1930.'

TASK 3: ODD ONE OUT

i) Here are 12 groups of words or phrases. In each group there is an odd one out. What do the three words have in common that the fourth does not have?

When you think you've found it, write a sentence or two explaining why you think it doesn't fit in with the others.

a Ford • BMW • Chrysler • General Motors

b Valentino • Fairbanks • Lindbergh • Bow

c AYAK • KIGY • NAACP • AKIA

d break-dancing • Charleston • Tango • Black Bottom

e Babe Ruth • Bobby Jones • Jack Dempsey • Charlie Chaplin

f mah-jong • crosswords • skateboarding • marathon dancing

g Armstrong • Harlem • Ellington • Waller

h bootlegging • Prohibition • racketeering • speakeasies

i laissez faire • New Deal • chicken in every pot • rugged individualism

j 1930 • 1932 • 1936 • 1940

k AAA • FBI • CCC • HOLC

l Franklin Roosevelt • Huey Long • Francis Townsend • Charles Coughlin

ii) Try to create your own 'odd one out' lists. Swap them with your friends.

TASK 4: QUESTION TIME

Look at these genuine GCSE questions carefully. Why not try to complete one, two or even all of them as a revision exercise? In brackets after each question, you will find the pages of this book where there is information that might refresh your memory.

- What were Hoover's economic policies? (pages 10–11, 64)
- How did Roosevelt's early life prepare him for a career in politics? (page 65)
- How far was Roosevelt <u>himself</u> responsible for his election victory in 1932? (pages 64–67)
- 'Hoover lost the Presidential election of 1932 *only* because of the Wall Street Crash.' Do you agree with this statement? Explain your answer. (pages 64–67)
- What was the New Deal? (pages 68–71)
- Explain why Roosevelt introduced the New Deal. (pages 64–71)
- 'Roosevelt replaced a *do nothing* government with a *do everything* government.' Do you agree with this statement? Explain your answer. (pages 68–75)
- Why was there opposition to the New Deal? (pages 78–79)
- Was the New Deal a success or a failure? Explain your answer. (pages 86–89)

Glossary

Alphabet agencies   The nickname given to the organisations and agencies set up as part of the New Deal.

Anarchist   A person who believes that countries should not be ruled by governments with set laws and rules. Instead, there is a system of cooperation where everyone rules themselves.

Anti-Flirt League   An organisation set up to protest against the 'outrageous' behaviour of young men and women, but in particular, flappers.

Anti-Saloon League   A Christian organisation that campaigned for a ban on alcohol.

Assembly line   A line of workers and machines in a factory assembling a product.

Atheist   A person who believes there is no God.

Beer Act   A 1933 government act that made the manufacture and sale of alcohol legal again.

Billboards   Huge roadside and city centre display boards carrying adverts for consumer goods.

Black Thursday   Thursday 24 October 1924 – the first day of the Wall Street Crash, when share prices fell faster and lower than at any other time before or since.

Bootleg   Alcohol brought in illegally from another country.

Bootlegger   A person who brings in alcohol illegally from another country.

Brain Trust   A group of men and women with fresh and exciting new ideas who worked for President Roosevelt.

Breadline   A long queue that waits for free bread, soup or blankets.

Cash and Carry Plan   A 1939 plan whereby Britain and France bought weapons and planes from America, as long as they collected them in their own ships.

Chaperone   Older person who accompanies and supervises a young person on a day (or night) out.

Communist   A person who believes that all economic activity (factories, farms, transport and so on) should be owned and run by the government for the benefit of everyone, and that all wealth should be divided equally.

Congress   The law-making body, or parliament, of the USA.

Constitution   A set of rules for the government of America, set out in the 18th century. Changes to these rules are known as 'amendments'.

Consumer goods   Products available to buy by the vast majority of ordinary people, such as watches, vacuum cleaners, cars, radios and so on.

Contemporary   Something from the same period of time.

Crazes   Short-lived fashion for an item of clothing, a leisure activity or similar. Sometimes called a 'fad'.

Democratic Party   One of the two main political parties in America. Seen as more sympathetic to the problems of the poor.

Dividend   Payment from the profits of a company to those who have shares in it.

Dust Bowl   A large area of farmland in which the soil was too dry and exhausted to grow good quality crops. Terrible dust storms hit this part of America as well, forcing many to leave their farms.

Economy Act   A 1933 government act that cut spending on government wages.

Emergency Banking Act   A 1933 government act that closed down all banks and only allowed the well-run ones to reopen.

Evolutionist   A person who believes in the theory of evolution.

Fireside chats   The nickname given to President Roosevelt's radio broadcasts in the 1930s.

Flapper   Usually richer, younger women who shocked older Americans with their independent behaviour.

Fundamentalist   A person who takes a literal or strict interpretation of a religion.

Gangster   A member of a criminal gang.

Great Depression   The very serious economic crisis that hit America after the Wall Street Crash. Too many goods were produced, not enough people bought them and millions lost their jobs. It lasted for most of the 1930s.

Hooverville   A shanty town made from old rubbish, where homeless people live.

Immigrants   People coming from abroad to live in a country.

Import duties   Taxes or charges put on goods imported (brought in) from foreign countries.

Infamous   Well known for doing bad things.

Investor   A person who buys shares in a company hoping to make a profit.

Isolationism   The idea that America should <u>not</u> play an important role in European problems and concentrate on what is happening in their own country.

Jazz   A type of music, started by Black Americans, with an exciting rhythm. It often involves improvisation.

Johnson Act   A law that banned American loans to any countries involved in wars.

Klonversations   Secret, coded language used by the Ku Klux Klan, a racist organisation.

Laissez faire   Literally means 'leave alone'. A policy, followed by the Republican Party in the 1920s, which meant that the government did not interfere too much in the lives of ordinary Americans.

'Lame duck months'   The period of time between November 1932 and March 1933 where old President Hoover continued work until new President Roosevelt took over.

Lend-Lease   A 1941 arrangement whereby America lent military equipment to Britain (and later Russia) free of charge.

Lynching   Hanging someone without a fair trial.

Mass production   Making goods in large numbers, usually on an assembly line.

Moonshine   Home made alcohol, often very poisonous!

Neutrality   Taking neither side in a war or dispute.

Neutrality Laws   The laws in 1935 and 1937 that were designed to keep America out of foreign wars.

New Deal   The name President Roosevelt gave to his economic recovery plan during the Great Depression.

Organised crime   Groups of people, often called gangsters, working together to break the law.

Overproduction   Producing too many goods.

Priming the pump   The idea that the government spends money to create jobs that, in turn, means people have more money to spend. Eventually, the government gets some of the money back by taxing wages.

Prohibition   The nickname for the ban on making and selling alcohol in America. In force from 1920 to 1933.

Racketeering   An illegal activity in which gangsters demand a payment from a businessman or a shopkeeper on return for protection (and a promise not to smash up their shop).

Red Scare   A period in the 1920s where many Americans feared a Communist (Red) revolution or an anarchist takeover.

Repeal   To annul a law.

Republican Party   One of the two main political parties in America. Seen as more sympathetic to wealthy people.

Rugged individualism   The theory that people should overcome their problems through their own hard work, not by receiving help from the government.

Segregation   The separation of a number of people from the main group, usually because of race or religion.

Shareholder   A person who owns a share of a company in the hope of making a profit.

Speakeasies   Illegal bars during the Prohibition era.

Speculation   Buying shares on the stock market, often with borrowed money, hoping for a quick profit.

Star system   Nickname for the system by which movie companies worked hard to publicise the celebrity lifestyle of the star, not just the film itself, in the hope of big box office receipts.

Stock market   The place where shares are bought and sold.

Supremacy   The belief that white people are better or superior to all other races.

Supreme Court   America's highest court of law. It has the power to overturn (get rid of) any decisions made by other courts and decide whether any new laws are legal or constitutional.

Tariffs   A charge or tax put on goods coming in from another country. Tariffs on foreign-made goods make them more expensive – so people usually buy home-produced goods.

Theory of evolution   An idea that humans developed slowly from single-cell creatures over millions of years. Opposite to the 'creation theory', which proposes that God made the world.

Underconsumption   Not buying the amount of goods that have been made.

Volstead Act   Set out punishments for breaking Prohibition laws and defined 'intoxicating liquor' as only liquid containing more than half a percent of alcohol.

Index